WHO'S WATCHING YOUR MONEY?

WHO'S WATCHING YOUR MONEY?

The 17 Paladin Principles for Selecting a Financial Advisor

JACK WAYMIRE

WILEY

JOHN WILEY & SONS, INC.

Published by John Wiley & Sons, Inc., Hoboken, New Jersey.
Published simultaneously in Canada.

Limit of Liability/Disclaimer of Warranty: While the publisher and author have used their best efforts in preparing this book, they make no representations or warranties with respect to the accuracy or completeness of the contents of this book and specifically disclaim any implied warranties of merchantability or fitness for a particular purpose. No warranty may be created or extended by sales representatives or written sales materials. The advice and strategies contained herein may not be suitable for your situation. You should consult with a professional where appropriate. Neither the publisher nor author shall be liable for any loss of profit or any other commercial damages, including but not limited to special, incidental, consequential, or other damages.

Author's Disclaimer: The information contained in this book is not investment advice and should not be used to make financial decisions such as asset allocation and money manager selection. We recommend you use the services of a quality advisor for assistance in making these decisions. Also, we do not recommend making any changes to your current financial strategy without consulting qualified advisors in advance.

For general information on our other products and services, or technical support, please contact our Customer Care Department within the United States at 800-762-2974, outside the United States at 317-572-3993 or fax 317-572-4002.

Wiley also publishes its books in a variety of electronic formats. Some content that appears in print may not be available in electronic books.

Library of Congress Cataloging-in-Publication Data

Waymire, Jack.
  Who's watching your money : 17 paladin principles for selecting a financial advisor / Jack Waymire.
    p. cm.
  ISBN 0-471-47699-4 (CLOTH)
  1. Finance, Personal—United States. 2. Investments—United States.
I. Title.
  HG179.W34 2003
  332.024—dc22

                                    2003015164

Printed in the United States of America

10 9 8 7 6 5 4 3 2 1

I want to thank my children,
Justin and Lauren,
for their patience, support, and understanding
during the three years it took me to complete this book.

CONTENTS

Acknowledgments

I would like to acknowledge the tremendous effort of several people. They sacrificed their personal time in order to assist me in writing this book. Without their help, this project never would have been completed. They are Debbie Freeman, Jennifer Seitz, M'Lisse Stone, and Gayle Greene.

PREFACE

Financial service observers and executives believe rebuilding investor trust is the financial industry's number one challenge. Consequently, financial services companies will spend hundreds of millions of dollars in this endeavor because they know your assets move on trust. In other words, you are not going to turn your assets over to an advisor or company unless you believe they possess a minimum level of integrity. Unfortunately, the trustworthiness of companies and professionals is very difficult to measure. Most investors take it for granted—a major mistake given recent headlines and the realities that are described in this book.

The real question facing the industry is whether it is willing to change its business practices to rebuild trust or use "spin" to convince investors it has changed its practices—yet changing as few business strategies as possible. History says the answer will be to spin new stories about change but continue to conduct business as usual. In fact, the spin has already started as companies re-engineer their advertising messages, public relations strategies, and sales presentations.

Trust began to erode when investors experienced losses of $7 trillion in the early 2000s. The erosion accelerated when the press began reporting numerous breaches of trust that included the financial industry, corporate executives, and accountants. Breach of trust is actually too soft when describing the industry's treatment of investors—outright fraud would be closer to the truth. A consequence of these inexcusable ethical lapses is reflected in a recent study indicating only 8 percent of investors currently believe the industry is trustworthy. This is an historic low by a large margin, which is the financial industry's number one challenge. Whatever trust is left will erode even further, when hundreds of class action lawsuits are filed seeking to recover some portion of the massive losses experienced in

2000–2002. Additional conflicts will be exposed daily because plaintiff attorneys will be much more aggressive compared to relatively passive regulators when pursuing their claims.

The critical question is still whether Wall Street can rebuild trust, using spin, and continue its old business practices. As you might imagine, that would be the industry's preference because current business practices are entrenched and profitable. New standards and business practices would cost billions of dollars and take years to implement. For example, in a new business paradigm, companies would only hire well-educated advisors, spend twelve months training them, and place them in apprenticeship programs with experienced professionals for one to two years before they begin giving advice to you. Then there would be continuous education programs during the year with proctored examinations, to increase knowledge and determine levels of proficiency. Advisors who did not maintain passing scores would be terminated or demoted to support positions.

Quality companies would also provide full disclosure to investors on all matters that impacted the performance, risk, and expenses of their assets. Honest disclosure is the foundation of trust because investors would have the data they need to make informed decisions. The issue is very straightforward: investors need competent, trustworthy advisors so they can maximize the probability of achieving their financial goals. However, like integrity, competence is also difficult to measure, but it could be made much easier with adequate disclosure.

There are just a bare handful of firms, out of thousands, that would commit to this level of professionalism. For 98 percent of the firms, it will be business as usual. The companies will tell the press, regulators, and investors what they want to hear; they will be hit with token fines for their abuses, they will wait out the bad publicity, and the result will be little or no change to their business practices. The dominant strategy for dealing with this debacle will be damage control. This will be reality for one simple reason: doing what is best for investors reduces their profitability. It is much more profitable to put hundreds of thousands of poorly trained, inexperienced advisors on the street selling Wall Street products as quickly as possible.

If you question the financial industry's willingness to put its need for profit ahead of your need to achieve your financial goals, think of another industry with a similar motivation. Wall Street is willing to destroy your financial health to maximize its profits; similarly, the tobacco industry is willing to destroy your physical health. Notwithstanding the warnings on packages of cigarettes, 25 percent of Americans still smoke and investors will still invest with low quality Wall Street firms. That is because, regardless of the downside, they still need the products. The users of tobacco products are addicted while investors who blindly trust Wall Street do not have the knowledge or time to manage their own assets. The tobacco industry knows this and so does Wall Street, which is why there is so little motivation to change. The catalyst for change has to be the buyers of the services and products because the seller will continue to practice old business models until there is a reason not to.

When I developed the Paladin Principles and wrote this book, I had one very simple goal in mind: to change the way Wall Street treats investors by changing the way investors select financial advisors. This one change will have a profound impact on Wall Street when it can no longer sell bad products through incompetent and untrustworthy advisors. For this goal to be achieved, we have to create a critical mass of investors who use the Principles for selecting advisors. If we do not, then you can be sure it will be business as usual. You will continue to be at risk that Wall Street's need for profits will supersede your needs to achieve your financial goals.

As a reader of this book, we need to work together to create the critical mass that will get Wall Street's attention. Therefore, I would ask you to recommend *Who's Watching Your Money?* to your family members, friends, and associates. This grass roots campaign to change the abuses we have experienced for decades is a critical part of the strategy to change Wall Street. We do not have the billions of dollars the industry pours into advertising, public relations, and lobbyists to promote and protect its interests. What we could have is even more powerful: the buying power of millions of investors who refuse to play by Wall Street's rules when their financial futures are at stake.

When you use the Paladin Principles to select quality financial advisors you will make it increasingly difficult for low quality advisors to earn the types of incomes they are used to. These professionals will have to make a choice: increase the quality of their services or leave the industry for greener pastures. Those who want to stay in financial services will pressure the companies they work for to provide the services and support they need to meet the demands of educated investors. This is the catalyst that Wall Street needs to change the way it treats investors—the very investors on whom it depends for its profits.

The bottom-line is: investors have to impact profits to motivate financial services companies to change their business practices. The Paladin Principles can do that if enough investors adopt its process.

INTRODUCTION

Two financial realities of nightmarish proportions are affecting current and future retirees in America. First, millions of people will not be able to retire when and how they want to. Second, additional millions have the even worse prospect of running out of assets late in life when they are impossible to replace. If either scenario describes your situation, your dream of the golden years and a secure, comfortable retirement has already become a living nightmare.

There is no question that Wall Street's greed and ethical lapses have badly damaged the dreams of millions of investors. Seven trillion dollars of net worth evaporated between March 2000 and December 2002, as the values of many 401(k) accounts and personal portfolios plummeted to less than half of their former values. The magnitude of these losses (and their cause) prompted Eliot Spitzer, the Attorney General for the State of New York, to call them the result of the biggest consumer scam in history. Several major Wall Street companies were fined $1.4 billion in June 2003 for the behaviors that produced the trillions of dollars in losses. However, the fine was a mere drop in the bucket when compared to the magnitude of the losses and the damage they did to the typical American who believed in Wall Street.

How did the financial services industry pull off the greatest consumer scam in history? Most investors have never been to the financial district in New York, much less talked to a Wall Streeter. However, they did depend on the advice of 650,000 advisors who market financial products and services. Investors trusted these professionals who worked for industry companies and marketed Wall Street–manufactured products, but they paid an enormous price for their blind trust. If you are among the millions who suffered these devastating losses, the reason this happened is simple—you trusted the wrong professionals and an investment process that was loaded with undisclosed conflicts of interest.

In 2002 the reasons for the stock market meltdown began to surface. Daily newspaper headlines revealed the shocking breaches of trust that occurred at every level of the investment process. Companies "cooked" their books by overstating revenues and understating expenses. CEOs received IPO shares as enticements to "achieve" the valuations manufactured by Wall Street analysts. Auditors looked the other way because their firms were paid millions of dollars in consulting fees. Analysts were paid seven- and eight-figure bonuses to tout the stocks of weak companies that generated substantial investment banking fees for their firms. The objectivity and integrity that you expected was totally absent as individual and corporate greed took precedence over the needs of individual investors.

You might ask, *where were the regulators when all of this was happening? Are they not supposed to be responsible for protecting the interests of investors from unscrupulous companies and advisors?* The unfortunate truth is that they were no help—they had their own conflicts of interest. The National Association of Securities Dealers, a self-regulatory agency, is more concerned with the needs of financial services companies than with those of investors. The other principal regulator, the Securities & Exchange Commission, does not have adequate resources to do its job, because politicians who oversee it receive million-dollar contributions from the financial industry each year to make sure it is underfunded. Wall Street is willing to spend hundreds of millions of dollars a year on lobbyists who protect its extraordinarily profitable franchise. It seemed like everyone, from politicians to company executives to personal financial advisors, had been reaping the rewards of the investment process. Everyone, that is, except the actual owners of the assets—investors like you.

Make no mistake: Personal greed and lapses of integrity are not new, and they are not going away. They simply go under cover until regulators, the press, and investors forget about them and move on to new issues. We have experienced similar scandals for decades, but they were usually viewed as aberrations—the personal greed of a few unprincipled individuals. However, the 1990s were a unique period of unprecedented excess by large numbers of companies and professionals. Perhaps this extraordinary decline in ethical standards is the reflection of a decade in which "spin" was more important than substance.

At the center of this unprecedented debacle are the financial advisors who developed personal relationships with you so they could market Wall Street's products and advice. You trusted the advisors with your financial futures—in particular, the assets you were depending on for secure, comfortable retirements. You trusted companies because you trusted their advisors who spent time building relationships with you. This trust was misplaced, however, and it was a primary contributor to the massive losses suffered by millions of investors.

Although we cannot blame advisors for the severe reduction in stock prices, we can hold them accountable for the advice they offered during those years. In down markets, their role is to help preserve the value of your assets by minimizing losses. In rising markets, their role is to produce competitive returns consistent with your tolerance for risk. Quality advisors influence investor decisions through sound advice, and that includes staying properly diversified during periods of market excess (up or down).

The relationship between investors and advisors has been the focus of my career in the financial services industry for the past 27 years. For 20 of those years, I was the president of two financial services companies that furnished investment services, financial products, and support services to thousands of personal financial advisors. In turn, these advisors worked with hundreds of thousands of investors.

I was in a unique position to observe the very different agendas that investors, advisors, and financial services companies bring to the relationship. For example, investors want competitive returns based on their goals and tolerances for risk. Advisors want quality lifestyles that require substantial amounts of income. The professionals' companies want to maximize profitability, executive bonuses, and stock valuations. Too often, these differing goals become the basis for major conflicts, and the losers are always investors because advisors control the relationships.

The bottom line is that you need significant performance from your assets to guarantee a comfortable future. This creates a major problem. Either you have adequate investment knowledge and time to manage your own assets, or you will hire professionals to do the work for you. Most individuals do not possess the necessary skills or time, so they seek help from advisors, believing that the "experts" will generate higher returns than they can produce on their own. Consequently, I strongly believe that the single most important decision you will ever make for the future performance of your assets is the selection of high-quality, personal financial advisors due to the considerable amount of influence or control they have over your decisions. Choose the right advisor and you will have more assets. Choose the wrong advisor and you will have fewer assets. It is that simple.

Selecting an advisor sounds straightforward enough, but the process is fraught with peril for two primary reasons. First, very few investors really know how to select quality advisors. You usually listen to sales presentations, the content of which is totally controlled by the professionals, and then use your "gut instincts" to pick the one you like the best. This process leads to a major source of risk that can destroy your financial future. The second source of peril is the broad range in the quality of advisors—great to terrible. Great advisors have excellent credentials and integrity; they help you achieve your financial goals. Terrible advisors have weak credentials and are nothing more than poorly trained sales representatives.

The fact is, the culture that dominates the financial services industry is based on selling, not advising. The most profitable companies and many of the highest-paid advisors are those that sell the most products or, put differently, control the largest amounts of your assets. Only a small percentage of advisors have risen above this culture and are really the trustworthy professionals you need to achieve your goals.

Now that the problem is out on the table, what can you do about it? Do not have any illusions about the industry fixing itself—it is making too much money using well-established practices to change anything. As long as you are willing to buy whatever the companies are selling, they have no reason to change their tactics or services. The bottom line is that the catalyst for change will have to come from outside the industry.

Ultimately there is only one solution: you must acquire enough knowledge to take responsibility for your own financial future. At a minimum, this means learning to select quality advisors for your assets. You may not be a money manager or an investment consultant, but you are the owner of the assets, the principal decision-maker, and the ultimate beneficiary.

The good news is that thousands of great advisors are available to help you achieve your financial goals. They have excellent credentials, based on years of education and experience, plus high levels of integrity and quality services; also, they are paid fees, just like other professionals. It is good to know that there are qualified advisors out there, but choosing one can be difficult.

First of all, great advisors are hard to find. They do very little marketing because they do not have to. They receive referrals from satisfied clients and other professionals. Or, they have taken on as many clients as they are capable of servicing and are not looking for more.

Once you find professionals you think are high quality, you have to know how to evaluate their credentials to make sure they are as good as they say they are. If you continually base your selections only on sales presentations and intuition, then you are destined to replace advisors every few years. Your financial future will eventually be damaged beyond repair because you have run out of time.

I wrote *Who's Watching Your Money?* to solve these problems for you and millions of investors just like you. It is important to note this is not an investment book. Thousands of books have been written on how to invest your own assets. However, our research indicates that only 16 percent of investors actually conduct their own research and make their own investment decisions. The other 84 percent of investors with more than $100,000 of investable assets use the services of Wall Street and advisors, especially after the meltdown in securities prices in the early 2000s. This book is written for the 84 percent.

The book describes the problems associated with finding, evaluating, selecting, and monitoring advisors. It describes the characteristics of lower-quality professionals and higher-quality ones, so you can tell the difference. The 17 Paladin Principles provide a summary solution that will dramatically increase the probability of your finding a quality advisor to help you attain a secure financial future.

It is my hope that you will use the knowledge and selection process described in this book to pick advisors whose core attributes are financial knowledge and trustworthiness. In addition, I would encourage you to tell your family members, friends, and associates about The Principles in this book, because as the quantity of knowledgeable investors increases, so will the quality of personal financial advisors.

There is no question that Wall Street only changes its culture when it is in its best interest. A critical mass of knowledgeable investors is just the catalyst that it needs to improve the quality and ethics of its distribution system—the professionals you depend on for advice.

Besides helping investors, this book is written to create positive exposure for thousands of outstanding investment professionals. Lower-quality advisors frequently overshadow these premiere advisors because they possess superior sales skills—after all, selling, not advising, is how they make their livings. You need to know these high-quality advisors exist because they are your solution.

Knowledge is power, and after reading *Who's Watching Your Money?*, you will be empowered to take control of your financial future before you run out of time—and the clock is ticking.

1

FINANCIAL REALITIES

Step one in your odyssey to accumulate and preserve substantial assets for retirement is to increase your awareness of several powerful realities that impact your investment decisions. Ignored, these realities will damage or destroy your financial future. You may have already experienced the financial impact of bad advice provided by incompetent investment professionals. Inevitably, the results are lost time and lost performance, both of which are irretrievable.

This chapter explains several of these realities and describes the only practical solution you have for the achievement of a lifetime of financial security.

The Wakeup Call

Any important objective, such as accumulating and preserving sufficient assets for retirement, requires a goal and a strategy. In fact, it is nearly impossible to achieve any type of complex, long-term objective without both. For example, suppose your goal is to accumulate $800,000 in retirement assets by age 65. If you do not have an effective strategy for generating the savings and performance needed to reach that figure, the goal will not be realized. You will be forced to choose between several onerous alternatives: deferred retirement, part-time employment, a reduced standard of living, or inadequate assets late in life.

It is an unfortunate reality that establishing long-term goals, executing complex strategies, and maintaining investment disciplines are not enjoyable tasks. They are frequently ignored, and investors hope the assets are there when they are needed. Then, when the problem is big enough, we force ourselves to acquire the knowledge to develop and execute a retirement strategy. However, by then it is often too late. There is an old adage in the financial services industry that most investors spend more time planning their next vacation than they do planning their financial futures. This is true for many people because they fail to realize that knowledge, goals, and strategy are the keys to a successful financial future.

You may be wondering why a personal commitment to knowledge is so important to the success of financial planning. It is because the accumulation of retirement assets has a powerful opponent that competes with your interests. That competitor is the financial services industry itself, and you cannot always trust the information that is provided by its representatives. The core problem is that there are conflicting goals. Yours is to maximize financial security, whereas the industry's goal is to maximize profits. An advisor's goal is to maximize personal income. All three goals must be achieved with your assets, which produces competing interests. It is critical that you understand the characteristics of this competitor, because only then can you learn to protect your assets from an industry that more often than not places its interests ahead of yours.

Friendship Is Risky

The financial services industry spends millions of dollars a year teaching advisors how to build friendly relationships with you. This is because decades ago, it learned that personal relationships facilitate the sale of its products and increase its retention rates: you are more likely to buy and less likely to terminate the services of someone you like. Consequently, friendship is a technique that advisors use for developing trust, which in turn helps them sell financial products. The problem occurs when industry-wide goals are achieved at your expense—for example, the investment excess of the 1990s that produced seven trillion dollars of losses in the early 2000s.

You are entering into a business relationship that is based on a fair exchange: You pay the industry's advisors for value-added services that help you improve the performance of your assets. Friendship is not part of this exchange. Consider it a bonus "after" your financial goals are achieved.

False Sense of Security

The financial services industry spends hundreds of millions of dollars a year on marketing the critical importance of three things: relationships, trust, and results. It has also hired hundreds of thousands of financial advisors and taught them to build personal relationships. This has been a successful business model for decades.

However, recent headlines are beginning to alert investors to the conflicts of interest that permeate the industry. Millions of investors are no longer as secure as they once were when they believed their assets were "in the right hands." At the center of the controversy are the professionals who represent the industry's companies, market its products, and develop trusting relationships with you.

You may feel comfortable with the financial advisor who currently controls or influences how you invest your assets in the securities markets. The critical question is whether this feeling is warranted by the competence and trustworthiness of a professional who puts your interests ahead of his or her own. A major risk is that your feelings have been influenced by years of advertising, brand names, structured presentations, and relationship skills, all of which have nothing to do with competence, trust, or results.

Awareness Is Power

You will be in a better position to take control of your financial future when you are aware of the powerful forces that impact your ability to accumulate and preserve retirement assets. If you have this knowledge, you will no longer be dependent on an industry that uses your assets to maximize its revenue and profit. Control also means that you are no longer susceptible to industry strategies that deliver unfulfilled promises.

Just think about the catastrophic consequences if the opposite were true—maybe you already have in the early 2000s. Lack of awareness transfers your power to an industry that has proven its willingness to compromise your financial future to satisfy its own needs.

Critical Financial Needs

There are three investment-related needs for retirement that, if you meet them, will produce a secure financial future:

1. Substantial assets that produce sufficient income to fund your lifestyle during retirement and provide financial security late in life.
2. Competitive returns that produce the assets.
3. Competent, trustworthy advice that produces the returns.

How Much Is Enough?

Most investors do not know how much money they will need for retirement or financial security late in life. This lack of awareness is a paradox because this target number is such a critical variable when planning for retirement. One easy way to determine the monetary figure is described in a 2002 Charles Schwab study. It concluded that you will need $230,000 of assets for every $1,000 of monthly income ($230 of assets for every dollar of monthly income, an annual payout rate of 5.2 percent during your retirement years). At $5,000 per month, you will need $1,150,000 of assets. At $10,000 per month, you will require $2,300,000. At $20,000, you will need to accumulate $4,600,000.

Longevity is one of the primary reasons that creates the need for substantial assets. According to the Annuity 2000 Mortality Table, the joint life expectancy of a couple age 65 is 92—a horizon of 27 years or more if you retire at age 65. There is a 25 percent chance one partner will live to age 97. Life expectancy has increased two or three years in just the past decade alone. You can thank modern drugs, genetic therapies, technology, and healthier lifestyles for this dramatic increase.

Pre- and early retirees are just beginning to recognize the financial implications of living longer. They will need substantially more asset value than their parents did if they want financial security late in life. In addition, they will have to generate higher returns and take more risk for as many as fifteen years after retirement to protect their principal and purchasing power. Running out of assets and returning to work at age 80 is simply not a viable strategy.

Competitive Returns

Your need for substantial assets drives the need for significant investment performance. This is based on the premise that millions of future retirees with a few hundred thousand dollars in their retirement accounts will have no way to "save" their way out of financial uncertainty. They will need significant performance in order to increase asset amounts—this is their only viable option.

Most of your annual increases in assets will come from performance and not savings because the principal amount in savings accounts is or will be larger than net income from salary and investment rates of return are higher than savings rates. As an example, suppose your one-year investment return on $300,000 was 12 percent, producing $36,000 in new assets. This compares to a savings rate of ten percent on your personal net income of $80,000, yielding $8,000 of new assets to invest. In this example, 82 percent of your increased assets comes from investment performance. As you can see, unless you have the unusual ability to save very large sums of money, performance is the critical component to a comfortable, secure retirement.

Competent, Trustworthy Advice

To achieve the performance you require from your assets, you will need competent advice from a professional whom you can trust. This person must possess the requisite knowledge and have access to sophisticated services in order to advise you on the optimum strategy for investing your assets. This means that the advisor must have substantial knowledge obtained from formal education programs and years of experience. The advisor must also provide objective, high-quality advice that puts your needs for assets and performance ahead of his or her personal need for income. Most importantly, the advisor must have a history of integrity. After all, how valuable is investment advice if you cannot trust it?

Advisors who meet these criteria are the exception rather than the rule. They are the most successful professionals in the industry, because all investors would like to use their services. They are the topic of this book.

What Are the Obstacles?

You have very specific financial goals. You need a specific asset value by a certain deadline in order to retire and enjoy financial security for the remainder of your life. Then you need a strategy that will maximize the chances of achieving that goal. Unfortunately, there are several daunting obstacles that stand in your way, and left unattended, they will destroy your plans.

You May Be an Obstacle

You may be your own worst enemy when it comes to selecting competent, trustworthy advisors for your assets. Why? Because you are susceptible to the overtures of an industry that make it easy to select and retain advisors for the wrong reasons. This susceptibility exhibits itself when you select advisors based on their carefully crafted sales presentations. It is also common to retain advisors for long periods of time, even when they are not delivering competitive performance for reasonable levels of risk and expense. It is always easier to maintain the status quo and hope that future performance will be better. "Hope springs eternal," as the saying goes, and the financial services industry is very skilled at marketing hope. It is an unfortunate reality that your hopes are in direct conflict with the industry's need to maximize profits for its companies and income for its advisors.

Bad Advice

Our research indicates that up to 84 percent of investors with more than $100,000 place their financial futures in the hands of investment advisors who have a broad range of credentials and capabilities.

Based upon my experience, the large majority of these advisors are not the competent professionals you think they are. Instead, they are representatives who are paid commissions to sell particular types or brands of financial products. When you hire inexperienced or poorly trained professionals, there is a high probability that you will receive bad or tainted advice.

This is one of your major obstacles. If you are going to entrust your financial future to a professional, you had better be sure that the professional is competent and worthy of your trust. The advisor must meet certain minimum standards, or you will pay a severe price later in life, often when it is too late.

Savings and Debt Rates

Another obstacle is your ability to save your way out of a retirement asset deficit. Baby boomers, the next generation to retire, have the lowest savings rates in history. This reality has been fueled by a number of contributing factors. The securities performance of the roaring '80s and '90s led many investors to reduce their savings rates, thinking the extraordinarily high returns would go on indefinitely. The same generation is also experiencing the highest debt in history, and discretionary income that could be going into savings accounts is diverted to interest and principal payments. High debt payments and low savings rates dramatically affect your ability to accumulate assets for retirement. If this describes your situation, your only recourse is to try to catch up by maximizing the performance of your assets.

Personal assets, held outside company pension plans, are a critical component of any retirement planning strategy. The Social Security Administration estimates that the average American of modest income derives 24 percent of retirement assets from qualified plans, 21 percent from Social Security, and 55 percent from personal assets and income. It will be very difficult for most Americans to retire with financial security if they are overly dependent on income from retirement plans or Social Security.

The extraordinary popularity of 401(k) plans in the '80s and '90s also increased your need for higher investment returns. Previous generations retired from companies that provided benefit plans with guaranteéd incomes for life. Underperformance was the employer's problem, and the company would make additional contributions to make sure that there were adequate assets for required distributions.

If you are a baby boomer, it is likely that you work for a company that sponsors a 401(k) plan and not a defined benefit plan. When you contribute pre-tax dollars to the plan, the company may or may not provide a matching contribution, and the amount of assets you will have for retirement is determined by the performance of the plan. In other words, unlike your parents, you are impacted by the performance of the plan's investments—just as you are in your IRA and other personal investment accounts.

Competitive performance is the only way you can adequately protect your lifestyle.

Erosion

Your need to produce competitive rates of return on your assets does not stop the day you retire. Your tolerance for risk will decline, but the need to produce high single-digit returns is still a reality. You will need performance to offset the four principal forms of erosion: distributions, inflation, and investment expenses. Rising longevity exacerbates this problem, because the longer you live, the more erosion you will experience, especially from inflation. Your only solution is to increase your assets by an amount that produces enough return to offset distributions, expenses, and the impact of inflation.

Complex Markets

Performance requires investment in stocks, bonds, real estate, and other types of assets that appreciate and/or produce income. According to Federal Reserve data, 75 percent of all retirement assets are invested in the securities markets because they do both. This brings another reality into play: the extraordinary complexity of the financial markets and your understanding of those markets.

Some of the smartest people on earth manage money, but even their track records are lower than the market averages a significant percentage of the time. When intelligent, experienced, educated, and focused specialists have trouble producing competitive returns, you get some idea of just how complex the securities markets really are.

Producing consistent, double-digit returns is exceptionally difficult when you are trying to predict the unpredictable. However, that is exactly what you need to do for a secure, comfortable retirement.

There are no "free lunches" when you invest in the securities markets. If you want to earn higher returns, you have to assume more risk. If you are risk-averse, then you have to accept lower returns. For example, if you are seeking higher returns, you will invest more of your assets in the stock market. If you are satisfied with moderate returns, you will invest in the stock and bond markets. If you are seeking low risk and are willing to accept lower returns, then you will invest in the short-term bond and cash equivalent markets. There is no way around this reality, even though investment-scam representatives say that they have discovered a way to achieve high returns for low risk—the ultimate free lunch that does not exist.

You will most likely have to earn at least a ten- to twelve-percent return during your working years and a seven- to nine-percent return during the first two-thirds of your retirement years to achieve your lifetime financial goals. Neither return can be achieved with 100 percent of your assets invested in bonds. A reality is that you will have to invest in the complex stock market to achieve these returns.

Time Commitment

The next obstacle is the amount of time that it takes to successfully invest your assets in the securities markets. A substantial amount of time must be devoted to developing outlooks, researching alternatives, making decisions, monitoring, replacing managers, and updating your analyses. It stands to reason that the investment of your retirement assets is not the place to take shortcuts when allocating your time.

Investing is a time-consuming process because there are so many choices, massive amounts of data, and continuous changes. If you are like most investors, you do not have sufficient time to analyze all of the data, make investment decisions, and monitor outcomes. This is because you are busy in your career or are enjoying retirement activities. It requires substantial discipline to devote several hours per week to investment activities—even more discipline than exercising or eating the right foods in moderation.

Investing may be your hobby, but there should be nothing casual about the accumulation and preservation of retirement assets. You need goals, a strategy, knowledge, and time to be a successful investor. If you do not possess all of these things, then you need a personal financial advisor.

Smart Decisions

Another potential obstacle is the constant pressure to make smart investment decisions with your assets. The pressure is constant due to the frequent changes that occur in the financial markets. Every mistake you make will reduce your future asset value as well as the time you have available to compound higher returns. For example, assume that you should have earned 12 percent in a particular year, but you earned only 7 percent. Because you have lost time and money, you now need above-average rates in subsequent years to offset the loss. The bottom line is that small amounts of underperformance equal large amounts of lost assets over long time periods.

The Impact of Insufficient Assets

There are also several realities related to having inadequate assets for retirement, and all of them are onerous. You already know what they are, and as you get closer to retirement, you will probably spend some sleepless nights worrying about them. Avoiding these realities means having sufficient assets to produce the income you need to maintain your desired standard of living for the rest of your life.

Deferred Retirement

According to several polls, boomers who are currently in their fifties say that they will not mind working past age 65. The reality is that they will not have a choice. They will have to continue working because they will not be able to retire and support their current lifestyles. In addition, their attitude about working longer will change as the aging process and health problems take their toll. At a minimum, the motivation, if not the physical ability, to work full-time declines with age.

Deferring retirement to age 70 or 75 increases the amount of time that you have to accumulate assets and compound higher rates of return. It also postpones the need to take distributions. If this is your best option (and it will be for millions of Americans), then you will have to adjust to this reality.

Part-Time Work

Another alternative to having insufficient assets is to supplement retirement income with part-time work. There will likely be a labor shortage as boomers begin retiring; you can take advantage of this shortage by working part-time. Assuming the activity is desirable, working part-time may be more palatable than deferring your retirement date because a higher portion of your time will be available for leisure activities.

Reduced Standard of Living

Reducing your current standard of living is another alternative that may be less onerous when compared to your other choices. The reduction process cuts expenses and may also free up assets that can be used to produce additional income. For example, you could sell your large expensive home, use part of the proceeds to buy a smaller, less expensive one, and invest the remainder in assets that produce retirement income.

Financial Insecurity

The impact of insufficient assets is most devastating late in life when you have no way to accumulate more—unless you are the heir to a significant fortune. It is at this stage that older retirees who have run out of assets become wards of the state or move in with their children. People who have been independent their entire lives are suddenly dependent on the generosity of others. Add a disabling illness to the equation, such as Alzheimer's disease, and you have a recipe for personal disaster.

Just the thought of this possibility produces a substantial amount of stress for millions of current and future retirees. The only solution is to take action as soon as possible—time delays make the task of accumulating assets that much more daunting.

You Need a Personal Financial Advisor

Your critical need for assets produces an equally critical need for performance, which creates a requirement for knowledge. This knowledge can only be provided by a personal financial advisor who is competent and trustworthy.

These needs, plus the complexity of the securities markets, are the principal reasons why 84 percent of investors seek the advice of professionals to help them make investment decisions. You expect that the advisor's education, experience, and full-time commitment will produce superior returns (net of all expenses) compared to what you could do on your own. In addition, the right advisor can help you overcome all of the obstacles that were described earlier in this chapter.

Quality Advisors

If you decide to outsource the work of investing, you are faced with another reality: most advisors sound good, but only a small percentage actually possess the qualities you need. Your challenge, as with researching and selecting your own investments, is to obtain enough reliable information to tell the good ones from the bad. Then you can select an advisor who is qualified to help you achieve your financial goals for retirement.

The best advisors comprise the upper echelon of the profession (less than five percent). They possess the competence and integrity you are looking for. They are well educated, have years of valuable experience, possess important certifications, belong to the right associations, and have clean compliance records.

Another 20 percent of advisors possess characteristics of both low- and high-quality advisors and are transitioning to the upper echelon. These professionals are currently acquiring credentials, gaining experience, and evolving from selling commission products to providing value-added advice for fees.

The remaining 75 percent of advisors are representatives who sell financial products for commissions. They add little or no value to the investment process because value is not their focus, nor is it the way they are measured or compensated. They recommend particular products as part of a sales process that is loaded with conflicts of interest, and it is up to you to identify them.

This tremendous range in advisor quality is not readily apparent and it makes sense for the industry to hide advisor ineptitude from you, because it knows that you would never knowingly turn your assets over to a weak advisor. Consequently, that is exactly what millions of investors do every year because they base their decisions on advisor-controlled sales presentations instead of more objective criteria.

Conflicts of Interest

Perhaps you blindly trusted the financial services industry to invest your assets in the past. The blinders have been removed, though, by the recent headlines that described the extraordinary conflicts that permeate Wall Street. Because you know that the industry is loaded with conflicts of interest—a long-standing problem that is now in the limelight—it is up to you to use that information to minimize its impact on your assets.

Whenever an advisor places his or her interests ahead of yours, there is a conflict. Inevitably, it means that the advisor is benefiting financially at your expense. The reality is that there will always be competing interests when one person can take advantage of another for personal gain—the problem is as old as time. The insidious part of the financial services industry is that it sells trust and then deliberately abuses it. Knowing this reality exists means that you have to be exceptionally careful when you rely on the advice of advisors for your financial future.

The Selection Process

The selection of quality advisors requires a completely objective process in order to gather the information necessary to compare several professionals to each other. You will also need to conduct an interview, because you should never use the services of an advisor without meeting him or her in advance.

This book will help you select quality advisors and avoid professionals who are not focused on your best interests.

Advisor Monitoring

Once you have selected a professional, it is critical that you monitor the quality of advice you receive for your assets. This means that you need benchmarks which accurately reflect your return objectives and tolerance for risk. Advisors must be held accountable for the quality of their services, just like other professionals.

Who's Watching Your Money? will help you develop monitoring systems that you can use for evaluating your advisor's services.

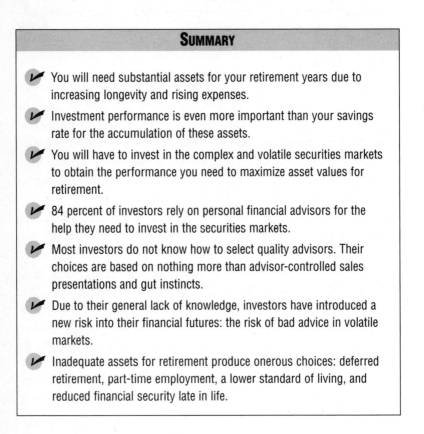

SUMMARY

✔ You will need substantial assets for your retirement years due to increasing longevity and rising expenses.

✔ Investment performance is even more important than your savings rate for the accumulation of these assets.

✔ You will have to invest in the complex and volatile securities markets to obtain the performance you need to maximize asset values for retirement.

✔ 84 percent of investors rely on personal financial advisors for the help they need to invest in the securities markets.

✔ Most investors do not know how to select quality advisors. Their choices are based on nothing more than advisor-controlled sales presentations and gut instincts.

✔ Due to their general lack of knowledge, investors have introduced a new risk into their financial futures: the risk of bad advice in volatile markets.

✔ Inadequate assets for retirement produce onerous choices: deferred retirement, part-time employment, a lower standard of living, and reduced financial security late in life.

2

TRUST

If you are the typical investor, you have never taken the time to acquire the specialized knowledge you need to invest assets on your own. Instead, you hire a personal financial advisor to help you earn the returns you need to achieve your financial goals. At the core of your relationship with a professional is implicit trust. If you are like most investors, you follow this professional's advice almost 100 percent of the time. You trust advisors to be knowledgeable, experienced, and honest. You trust advisors to use their expertise to help you achieve your financial goals. You trust advisors to deliver the performance that they promise. You trust advisors to always place your interests ahead of theirs. These are reasonable expectations when you turn your assets over to financial professionals and the companies they represent.

However, according to state securities regulators, stockbrokers and other professionals are increasingly turning to deception to keep their commissions up in the down market of the early 2000s. Only the sales practices of insurance agents, not licensed to sell securities, were rated more deceptive. Susan Wyderko, director of the SEC's Office of Investor Education and Assistance stated, "The kinds of frauds we are seeing are where investors are promised higher returns than they could ordinarily expect to receive from legitimate investments." Some important questions arise. Does the advisor whom you selected actually deserve your trust? Does the advisor really have sufficient competence and integrity to help you earn the returns you need to achieve your financial goals? Is the advice objective, devoid of the conflicts of interest that seemingly permeate the financial service industry? The unfortunate reality is that you will not know the answers to these questions until years later when you evaluate the results using hindsight. If you selected the wrong advisor, you have lost both years and thousands of dollars to underperformance. Your only solution is to find a new advisor to trust, and "hope" that your next experience is a good one.

This chapter is dedicated to the importance of trust when turning your assets and financial future over to a personal financial advisor.

Trusting Yourself

Before focusing on the trustworthiness of your advisor, you should think about trusting your own knowledge and judgment. As the investor, there are certain decisions only you can make. It is important to objectively assess your own qualifications with regard to the investment of your assets. Do you have a basic understanding of the securities markets and investment principles? Do you know how to select managers who have a high probability of producing competitive returns in the future? Do you know how to diversify assets to minimize the risk of large losses? Do you know how to evaluate performance? The less you know, the more dependent you will be on the advice of the professional. If you select the wrong advisor, this translates to even higher risk.

Decision Process

Another type of self-evaluation is your decision making process. Do you tend to make quick decisions based on your intuition, or are you more analytical and thoughtful? Do you have the time, motivation, and resources to do the investment work yourself, or do you delegate it? Do you take time to do your homework and compare your choices, or do you select the first alternative that looks good? The answers to these questions will determine the risk level of the process that you use for selecting an advisor.

If you are the intuitive decision maker, then adopting the structured process recommended in this book will be a challenge. You will have to learn to resist the temptation to make subjective decisions that are easy for you. Intuitive decision making must be replaced with research, comparisons, and analysis. After all, you only have a fixed number of years in which to achieve your financial goals.

Knowledge and Judgment

There are only two ways to acquire knowledge: education and experience. You are way ahead of most investors if you have educated yourself by taking classes that provide investment knowledge. Experience, sometimes referred to as "the school of hard knocks," is acquired differently. You may have increased your investment knowledge using a process of trial and error. You learned from your mistakes and, over time, began making wiser decisions for your assets.

Judgment is very different from knowledge. Whereas knowledge can be acquired in a classroom and over time, judgment is more of an art. For example, judgment involves analyzing two money managers and picking the one who will produce the best returns for your assets. Warren Buffett has judgment. So does John Templeton. However, as in any field of art, there are only a few great artists. For the rest of us mere mortals, judgment is the development of sound strategies coupled with the discipline to stick to them during the inevitable roller coaster rides experienced in the securities markets.

You should make an objective assessment of your knowledge and judgment pertaining to investments. If you rate yourself at the low end of the scale, you must be even more cautious about whom you trust when selecting an advisor—your implicit trust level will be very high. If you are at the high end of the investment knowledge scale, you may be more involved in the investment decisions for your assets and be less dependent on the quality of the advisor.

Emotions and Money

Money can have a profound impact on our emotions. For example, high investment returns and asset values produce strong positive feelings that include satisfaction, security, and confidence. This is the primary reason why we spend more when the stock market is producing substantial returns—we feel wealthier, even if the wealth is only on paper.

When returns are negative and markets are down, we spend less money—we feel poorer. Most of us have feelings of fear, anxiety, and depression. These emotions are triggered by the lack of control over events that produce rising and falling markets. The unpredictable fluctuation of returns is the main source of anxiety for most investors.

You cannot control the financial markets, but you can control the quality of your advisor. Learning to select quality professionals is much easier than acquiring the knowledge you need to invest in the securities market. Once you have a quality advisor, the volatility of the markets becomes more manageable and less worrisome.

The Decision You Cannot Delegate

There is bad news for investors who prefer to delegate all of the decision making to investment professionals. You have to be the decision maker for at least one of three choices: securities, money managers who pick securities, or personal financial advisors who help you select managers. If you are uncomfortable researching securities or analyzing and selecting managers, your only alternative is to hire an advisor to do the work for you. This is the most frequent solution for millions of investors.

The selection of an advisor is the only decision you cannot delegate. All other decisions for your assets can be delegated to advisors and money managers.

One Personal Financial Advisor

Because most investors do not have a functional process for selecting quality advisors, they have adopted a counterproductive solution. Inexplicably, they have concluded that the risk of making a bad decision is reduced when they hire several advisors. These investors divide their assets among multiple professionals and somehow feel safer. They reason that a bad advisor can only impact a portion of their financial futures. This is a badly flawed strategy for several reasons:

- There is a high probability that overall performance will suffer because there will be a lack of coordination among multiple advisors for asset allocation and manager selection.
- The higher performance from the recommendations of quality advisors will be offset by the lower returns of inferior advisors.
- You will pay higher fees because you will miss out on discounts that are based on asset amounts per advisor.
- You will have to personally coordinate the strategies of multiple advisors, an endeavor for which you may have neither the time nor the knowledge.

The real solution is to hire one quality advisor. You want someone whom you can trust with all of your assets. It is the financial professional's job to be the coordinator and diversify your assets among several money managers with different styles. This way, you can achieve maximum diversification and performance while minimizing fees.

Trust and Gut Instincts

Millions of investors rely on their gut instincts when making hiring decisions that are based on the sales presentations of advisors. If you choose to use this subjective process, be advised that this one decision may very well determine your standard of living and financial security during the 20 to 40 years of your retirement.

After having dealt with thousands of advisors, I know that you need more than just gut instincts to make this crucial decision. Selecting advisors using only your intuition is extraordinarily dangerous and should be avoided at all costs.

Gut Instincts

Trusting your gut instincts, or intuition, is the "easiest" way to hire a professional; it is just not a very smart way. You do not have to take time to gather information, evaluate it, and compare advisors. You may rely on referrals from friends or you may listen to a few presentations and make an intuitive decision to hire the professional who sounds the best. This process for selecting professionals is fraught with peril when you understand that there is a tremendous range in quality among advisors—a range that is never seen in sales presentations.

Hiring an advisor using a subjective process is the number one reason that millions of disappointed investors change advisors every two to three years. Intuition is subjectivity in its purest form, and even if you believe your intuition is above average, you must limit its use. Your financial future is far too important to leave to chance—there is enough of that already in the securities markets.

Thinking Versus Feeling

Financial industry training programs teach listening skills to advisors. They are taught to listen for two key words that investors use during their initial interviews with prospective advisors: *think* and *feel*. Your use of these two words enables the advisor to determine whether you will use a more objective process ("I think") or a more subjective process ("I feel") in your decision making.

Well-trained sales professionals will immediately adapt their approaches to the word you choose. Their strategy is to integrate this word into their presentations so that they are using the same words and phrases as you. Their goal is to create a trusting relationship as quickly as possible. For example, when an advisor acknowledges your fears (feelings) about investing in volatile stocks, it is designed to create a feeling of security. The advisor wants you to feel that your concerns are understood.

The "I think" investor asks carefully formulated questions designed to obtain information about an advisor's background and skills. The right questions uncover conflicts of interest, amounts of compensation, future service levels, and other information that is vital to know before making a selection.

Feelings should be part of the selection process, but only after you have evaluated all of the information you need to make a quality selection. When two advisors are equally qualified, you can pick the one you like the best. In other words, subjectivity follows objectivity, but objectivity is the foundation of the selection process.

Trust and Incompetence

In a perfect world, there would be only competent advisors whom you could implicitly trust with your assets. They would have the knowledge you expect them to have, and they would use it to help you achieve your financial goals. Unfortunately, we do not live in a perfect world. In the real world, advisors have to earn livings and companies have to produce profits, and they need your assets to accomplish their goals.

Financial services companies can generate higher profits when they field large sales forces for their products. Consequently, whether advisors are competent or not is secondary to their need to produce profits. Competent advisors are more expensive than incompetent advisors, due to higher training and support costs. It is up to you to determine the competency of advisors before entrusting them with your financial future.

Incompetence Increases Risk

Incompetence is an insidious form of risk. Well-meaning people can be incompetent. Nice people can be incompetent. Your friends and family can be incompetent. Members of your church or country club can be incompetent. Incompetence can destroy your dream of a secure retirement. Incompetence is difficult to identify and measure for the average investor because most professionals have more investment knowledge than you. They appear to be experts and their advice sounds reasonable.

Two important variables influence the risk level of your investment strategy: one is the inherent volatility of the securities markets, and the other is the quality of advice you receive when investing in these markets. When you combine volatile markets and incompetent advice, the risks to your assets increase dramatically.

The Real Impact of Bad Advice

The financial impact of incompetent advice is rarely measured, but it is very real. Think about the performance of the stock market in 1999 when the Standard & Poor's 500 Index was up 21 percent. Now consider the performance of the equities in your portfolio. Let us say that they were up 15 percent. If your assets took the same risk as the market, the underperformance of six percent was the result of incompetent advice—the professional recommended underperforming money managers. Six percent on a hypothetical $300,000 portfolio is $18,000 that is gone forever.

Incompetence can cost you a lot of money, even when the performance differences are very small. If you compound underperformance of two or three percent per year over 10-, 20-, or 30-year time periods, your losses could be in the hundreds of thousands of dollars. The lost dollars may be the difference between a quality retirement and one filled with compromises.

Trust and Integrity

Sophisticated investors consider integrity the most important trait in a financial advisor, according to a broad survey of the affluent by Click Communications in Chicago. It ranked as more important than performance results, breadth of services, fees, or personal recommendations. Common sense dictates that you should only trust advisors with integrity. Advisors must place your need to achieve financial goals ahead of their need to make comfortable livings—they win when you win. Your challenge is to determine levels of integrity when evaluating advisors.

Honesty

A very high percentage of all advisors are honest. They are simply doing what is required of them to keep their jobs and provide quality lifestyles for themselves and their families. Most investors would do the same thing in their position. The process is harmful to your interests because advisors are achieving their goals with your assets, and frequently at your expense. The critical question is: *Which are more important: your needs, their needs, or the needs of the companies they represent?*

Something illegal has to happen before advisors are judged dishonest, and nothing is illegal about placing their interests ahead of yours; in fact, it is an industry-wide practice. Integrity is a highly personal issue for advisors, and it takes an extremely high standard of personal ethics for them to put your needs first—especially when it impacts their income.

Trust and the Advisor's Company

Most investors find it easier to trust advisors who work for the name brand companies they see on television. However, brand names have very little to do with the quality of advice you will receive from the professional. As evidenced by recent headlines, it seems that major companies have more conflicts of interest than some smaller companies or independent advisors.

Advisors—not the companies they work for—are responsible for determining your needs and recommending suitable investment solutions. The firms may review your profile and their advisors' solutions, but they are not otherwise involved in the quality or appropriateness of the proposals. The advisor is supposed to know you better than the company does.

On this basis, advisors working for brand name companies must meet the same standards of trust as advisors who do not work for companies with high name recognition.

Trust and Three Types of Advisors

Three types of advisors work in the financial services industry: consultants, planners, and representatives. It is important to note that titles can be misleading because there are no industry regulations that govern titles or roles. For example, anyone can be called a financial consultant or planner.

Financial Consultants

Financial consultants provide several professional services that help you invest your assets with money managers. Their primary services include development of investment strategy, asset allocation, manager selection, portfolio monitoring, performance reporting, service meetings, and written investment policy.

I believe that consultants are the most trustworthy type of financial advisor for five reasons:

1. They have the most investment knowledge.
2. They are fee-based, so they work for you and not the product companies.
3. They do not market canned investment solutions.
4. They have fewer conflicts than other types of advisors.
5. They provide performance reports so you know the results of their advice.

Financial Planners

There are good planners and there are bad planners. Good planners market a comprehensive, high-quality service and charge a fee. Bad planners market a manipulative service that is used to develop relationships with investors and gain access to their assets. They typically produce low-quality plans that have little or no real value. The goal of these disreputable planners is to earn substantial amounts of commissions when you implement their planning recommendations. The quality of the plan is secondary to the sale of the product.

Many low-level planners offer their services for "free" because they are paid commissions by third parties and not you. Others charge a nominal fee ($100 to $200) and receive the bulk of their compensation from commissions derived from product sales. You should be extremely cautious when trusting services of this type. It pays to remind yourself that there is no such thing as a free lunch—you get what you pay for.

As discussed in Chapter Eight, high-level financial planners have the credentials and specialized knowledge to provide quality services that are based solely on your needs. They charge a fee for their service that reflects its value. This is the only type of professional whom you want to provide planning services that will impact your ability to retire.

Financial Representatives

Financial representatives make their livings by selling investment products for commissions. These products include mutual funds, annuities, life insurance, and brokerage services. They are the least knowledgeable of the three types of professionals, and they add the smallest amount of value to the overall investment process.

You might be wondering how low-quality advisors make a living in today's increasingly competitive marketplace. It is very simple. First, they typically sell products to inexperienced investors who have less to invest and who are less aware of the conflicts that surround financial representatives. Second, they are very good at building relationships to win trust. Third, they use sales skills to convince you to buy the products. Finally, they rely on sales volume. If advisors talk to enough prospects, they know that a certain percentage will invest based on their presentations.

If you are an investor with less than $100,000 in assets, you are particularly vulnerable to this type of advisor.

Trust and the Agreement

The service agreement is another way to evaluate the trustworthiness of the advisor and the advisor's company. You might think that a service agreement is just what it sounds like—a document that describes the services and pricing of the financial advisor. Think again. Most agreements are carefully drafted to protect the service provider and to obscure details that require disclosure. Insurance company documents are the epitome of obscurity, closely followed by the prospectuses of mutual fund companies. In both cases, relatively uncomplicated information is deliberately buried in a blizzard of technical and legal jargon. If you are wondering why, think about who wins when the details of the relationship are blurry.

One-Way Agreements

Many agreements are drafted with the sole intent of protecting advisors and their companies from as much liability as possible. If you read the agreement, you may determine that they are liable for outright acts of fraud—that is, if you can prove it beyond a reasonable doubt. The company will maintain that all other acts were committed with your best intentions in mind, and any mistakes were human error, for which they are not liable.

When I entrust my financial future to an advisor, I have certain expectations. For example, I expect suitable investments, attention to detail, timely communication, and full disclosure of issues that impact my financial interests. When I read an agreement indicating that the advisor is only responsible for "best efforts" and not required to meet my expectations, I have some serious concerns. This does not mean that I want guaranteed returns, but it does mean I want quality recommendations free of any potential conflicts of interest. When mistakes cause serious harm to your financial future, you should expect someone to be responsible for those mistakes.

Legalese

I would not hire an advisor or purchase a product from a company if I were presented with an agreement written in barely comprehensible legal language. If I need an attorney to review the document and provide me with findings, I will exclude that advisor from the selection process—or let the advisor pay the legal fee. Every advisor and company is capable of developing agreements that can be easily understood by you.

Voluntary Disclosure

A sound agreement contains voluntary disclosures designed to make you more comfortable with the advisor relationship. Your comfort level should be an important goal for the advisor and the financial services company—it builds trust. Disclosure about the advisors' compensation, affiliated companies, proprietary products, services covered by the agreement, liability for mistakes, and other important details that impact your level of trust should be included. You should be wary of agreements that do not include this information.

The Fine Print

If you are like most investors, you hire professionals and make investment decisions without carefully reading the legal agreements or prospectuses that describe the relationships. After all, you trusted the advisor enough to select him or her, so there is no reason to scrutinize the agreement. This is a big mistake. You must read the fine print to obtain the details of the relationship.

You will have no one to blame but yourself when you find that the expenses are higher than you thought, the investments are more risky, or there are substantial penalties for early withdrawal. Keep in mind that many advisors and companies do not want you to read their agreements; this is why they are designed to be difficult to read in the first place.

Trust and Track Records

Virtually all advisors would like you to hire them on the basis of their sales presentations. When asked about a personal track record, they will profess not to have one. They do not have a record which documents results because the client has acted as the decision maker—therefore, the success rate varies. All of their clients have different strategies and results.

Advisors who propose particular strategies for your assets will have a track record that is comprised of the cumulative performances of the various money managers in the proposal. They may also provide references that "document" their results. Neither one is a real track record because the advisors control the information after the fact. They used hindsight to pick managers and they selected references who would make positive statements about them.

Advisor Resistance

Advisors are in denial about the impact of their influence over your decisions because it is self-serving. Rarely is so much trust placed in practitioners who deny having any documented record of their accomplishments—especially practitioners whose decisions impact the financial futures of millions of people. This may explain why so many incompetent personal financial advisors can survive in the industry. They have made the measurement of the quality of their advice difficult to obtain.

Manager Performance

As mentioned, some advisors may provide you with money manager track records and represent them as their own. In other words, they recommend managers for your assets and use these track records to document the quality of their own services. In effect, they are saying that they are quality advisors because they recommend quality managers. However, the track records of managers have little or nothing to do with the quality of the advisor. Any advisor can select high-performing managers after the performance has occurred.

Hindsight Is Always 20/20

It is a near certainty that the manager track records included in the advisor's sales proposal do not represent the actual performance of their clients. The managers in the proposal were selected after the performance occurred, so the advisor had the benefit of 20/20 hindsight. Consequently, it is easy for an advisor to select the managers with the best track records. It should not be a surprise when their recommendations involve excellent track records. It *would* be a surprise if they did not.

Future Performance

Any advisor who guarantees future performance is in violation of securities regulations. There are no guarantees when you invest in the securities markets, because no one can accurately predict future returns—not even the "real experts." In fact, the SEC requires a disclosure on manager track records stating that "past returns are not indicative of future returns."

One way some advisors provide "sales" guarantees is to show you the track records of managers and imply that the returns are what you can expect in the future. This is the primary reason why "hot" managers attract so much money so quickly—investors are being sold on the idea that the future will be like the past. Track records are not guarantees. In fact, there is a low probability that excellent returns will be repeated. Never trust anyone with your assets on the basis that they can predict or guarantee future investment returns.

Trust and Conflicts of Interest

All financial advisors, regardless of what they call themselves, have potential conflicts of interest. In general, a conflict of interest occurs whenever advisors put their interests ahead of yours. The best way to think about conflicts of interest is to think in the context of competing interests. Whenever your interests collide with the interests of the advisors or the companies they represent, you have a potential problem, and they have a tremendous advantage. The advantage is a result of their influence over your choices and decisions. The only way you can protect yourself is with knowledge.

Frequent Conflicts

A few of the most frequent conflicts are as follows:

- Advisors sell you products manufactured by their own companies, even though the performance is inferior to other investment alternatives. For example, a professional from Acme Financial sells you an Acme mutual fund.
- Advisors sell you low-quality products to earn higher commissions.

- Advisors exchange one product for another for the sole purpose of generating a new commission.
- Advisors receive compensation that is not disclosed to you before or after the sale.
- Advisors are new to the industry, but do not disclose this information.
- Advisors have poor compliance records, but do not disclose this information.

Trust and Compensation

Any type of compensation (fee or commission) has the potential to generate a conflict of interest. It occurs whenever advisors are in a position to earn varying amounts of income based on their investment recommendations. Advisors have to make important choices when faced with potential conflicts on a daily basis, which is why integrity is such an important selection criterion. You want professionals who make good choices that are in your favor.

There is also the issue of your perception. For whatever reason, fees seem "real" and commissions do not. Fees are deducted from your accounts and you can see them, while third parties pay commissions directly to your advisor's company and you do not see them. Examples of third parties include mutual fund and annuity companies. Several types of commissions are difficult to identify unless your advisor voluntarily discloses them to you. A consequence of this payment method leads less knowledgeable investors to believe that the services they receive are free because the advisor said so.

Experienced investors know that nothing is free and that the product companies pass their compensation expenses on to them in the form of higher fees. Every penny of compensation that advisors receive, whether it is a fee or a commission, comes from you.

Paid in Advance

Sophisticated investors with larger asset amounts will not pay for financial advice years in advance. This is why they do not place their assets with advisors who work for commissions. These investors pay for services as they are rendered—for example, through the payment of a quarterly fee. That way, the professionals have to provide continuous services that meet expectations or risk losing future revenue if you terminate their services. If this happens, they have to refund any unearned fees.

Professionals have no incentive to provide ongoing services to you when they are paid commissions that are equal to years of fees in advance. For example, a one-time commission of five percent is equal to five years of one percent fees. In addition, they have no losses when you terminate their services, because they have already been paid, and there are no refunds.

Full Disclosure

It is easier to trust advisors who are willing to disclose the total compensation they receive for their services. It is a crucial part of your relationship with professionals to know what you are paying and what you receive in return for that expense. Advisors who refuse to disclose the information should not be trusted with your assets. If they are hiding compensation, what else might they be hiding? In an ideal relationship, the professional volunteers this information.

Trust and Personal Relationships

We all interact with various professionals: CPAs, attorneys, physicians, dentists, architects, veterinarians, and others. Rarely is it important to like them before you hire them. You use their services because they have specialized expertise that can help you complete work, solve problems, or achieve important personal goals.

A far different standard applies to the relationship that you have with your financial advisor. The basis for your selection may be completely subjective. This particular type of professional is exposed to some of your innermost thoughts, fears, and aspirations in a way that very few "outsiders" ever will be.

The Personable Advisor

The financial services industry has done its homework and understands the relative importance of relationships when you select an advisor. Consequently, the industry has built a large part of its sales strategy around developing and managing client relationships. One aspect of this strategy is to hire professionals who are personable and then train them to develop relationships. However, advisor personalities have nothing to do with competency and integrity. In fact, relationships can be a source of manipulation, and you should be very cautious when using them as a basis for entrusting an advisor with your financial future.

Trusting People You Know

Just because you know an advisor does not mean that you should entrust this individual with your assets. In fact, someone you know should be given additional scrutiny to make sure that your selection process is not tainted by subjective feelings. A good question to ask yourself is whether your current advisor won your assets based on the relationship or on an objective evaluation of his or her credentials. Trusting a professional you know can be more dangerous than selecting a professional you do not know.

Trusting People You Like

Hiring a professional you like can also be more dangerous than hiring a "stranger" whom you neither like nor dislike. Not only can your objectivity be compromised by your feelings, but business relationships with friends can also be difficult to terminate if they fail to meet your expectations. When it comes to your assets, trust should only be based on the competence and integrity of the individual, the quality of service, and total expenses. There is increased risk to your financial future when advisors become friends.

"Like" Does Not Equal Safety

If you are similar to most investors, you intuitively trust people you like, and you feel safe with people you trust. However, when it comes to your financial future, you should only feel safe when you know that a competent professional with high integrity is advising you on your assets. This knowledge should be based on an objective evaluation of the advisor's backgrounds and skills. Anything less and you are jeopardizing your financial future. "Likeability" allows advisors to use their sales skills, rather than competency and integrity, to win your assets.

Trust and Sales Presentations

Competence and integrity are the two most important characteristics you should look for in an advisor. Unfortunately, both are difficult to identify and measure, especially when your only source of information is a sales presentation. Can you trust the information in presentations when advisors control 100 percent of the content and their principal purpose is winning the relationship and your assets?

Sales Culture

First, it is important for you to recognize that the dominant culture in the financial service industry is sales and not advice. Hundreds of thousands of professionals sell investment products in the form of separate accounts, mutual funds, and annuities. You rely on advice from professionals who are actually the sales forces of companies that manufacture financial products. The sales culture of the industry creates an important trust issue when your primary source of information is the advisor's sales presentation. Are you being provided with complete, accurate data, or information that has only one purpose—to make the advisor look good? Rarely does the information in presentations meet the dual criteria of completeness and accuracy; therefore, its trustworthiness is highly suspect.

When you rely on sales presentations as your primary input for selecting advisors, you are allowing professionals to control all of the information you will use to evaluate knowledge and integrity. If the professionals have anything in their backgrounds that would negatively impact your impression, it will be deliberately left out. That is the principal danger of advisor-controlled information, and there is a substantial risk of hiring the wrong professionals when you base your selections on sales presentations.

One additional observation: disreputable advisors use verbal presentations, rather than hard copy, with strong representations that can be denied later. For this reason, it is critical that all information that will influence your decision making be in writing.

What You Want to Hear

There is an old saying: "If it sounds too good to be true, it usually is." You should apply this adage to a high percentage of what you hear from financial advisors. Advisors verbalize what they think you want to hear, so their presentations usually revolve around maximizing performance while somehow controlling your exposure to risk. They know investors want both, and their job is to convince you they can optimize this relationship better than their competitors.

Advisors are also very aware of what you do not want to hear. For example, investment risk is frequently understated because investors do not want to deal with that reality. They want to hear about the upside, not the downside. This is the equivalent of not wanting to hear about health risks from your doctor or mortality from your life insurance agent.

References Are Usually Worthless

References are rarely worth much and should not be relied on for the selection of advisors, especially if they represent the professionals' track record. All advisors have clients who have become friends, and these friends are willing to vouch for their qualifications, whether accurate or not. For all you know, you are talking to a relative of the advisor. It stands to reason that the less qualified the professional, the more he or she may try to win your assets with friendly references.

Referrals Can Be Dangerous

Many investment professionals network with other professionals as their principal strategy for obtaining new clients. Their most frequent type of networking is with the CPA community, which refers thousands of clients a year to financial advisors.

It is risky to automatically trust a financial services professional just because you trust the CPA who made the referral. You might feel that there is no need to evaluate advisors who are recommended by people you trust; however, there is substantial risk when you have no idea what the referral source's selection criteria are in relation to your own.

Trust and Telephone Solicitation

High-quality advisors who are competent and trustworthy do not solicit business over the telephone from investors they do not know. They use the telephone for setting appointments. Only new or lower-quality advisors, usually selling inferior products for high commissions, work this way.

You should never turn your assets over to advisors whose solicitation process is conducted over the telephone. A simple rule is to never select advisors sight unseen. The minimum age of an advisor is just 18, and you cannot determine age, much less other important credentials like experience, over the telephone. Just remember, you might be talking to a 19-year-old with a deep voice.

Trust Must Be Earned

Most investors hire an advisor, give this individual control over their assets, and wait two or three years to determine whether their hiring decision was a good one. During those years of reviewing investments and performance, you should be building a trust scorecard for your advisor in areas that are important to you. An advisor who continues to meet your expectations for results and service should be considered increasingly trustworthy. You might reward your advisor by placing additional assets with him or her, allowing more discretion over those assets, or giving referrals to family, friends, and associates.

Every disappointment you experience should also chip away at the foundation of trust until it eventually crumbles and you seek a new advisor.

See Versus Hear

"Trust what you see, not what you hear." This saying could have been written to describe the process for selecting and entrusting an advisor with your financial future. When what you hear and what you see diverge, you have just been given a warning which must be investigated.

For example, assume that you review your monthly brokerage/custodial statements and quarterly performance reports and they show that your assets are growing very slowly, while the financial markets are performing at a more robust pace. You ask your advisor about this anomaly and are told that your stocks are different from the other ones that are performing better. You are also told not to worry, that your advisor is on the job, monitoring your investments. But this is the very same advisor who recommended the managers who picked the stocks that are not performing as well as the markets.

This is not a trustworthy advisor, because your concerns were not adequately addressed. If you trusted what you read in the reports, you would know that what the advisor said was self-serving, designed to avoid termination.

Probation

No matter how much advance due diligence you conduct on your advisors, you will never establish complete trust before hiring them. This level of trust will develop over time as your advisor demonstrates the ability to help you achieve your financial goals. If you are like most investors, you will probably test a new professional relationship with a portion of your assets. For example, an investor with $800,000 of liquid assets might initiate a relationship with a new advisor by allocating only $200,000. The investor allocates the remainder to multiple advisors during the probationary period, which is not ideal. However, it may be the more conservative alternative if you are unsure of the advisor's competence and integrity. The better solution is to do a thorough evaluation of the advisor's credentials. After determining competence, you can then make him or her responsible for 100 percent of your assets and the achievement of your financial goals.

Bull and Bear Markets

Building a trusting relationship with advisors can be affected by current market conditions. For example, the advisor may seem smart, and therefore trustworthy, in bull markets. However, the advisor appears dumb, and therefore untrustworthy, in bear markets. You should not give advisors credit for bull markets, nor should you penalize them for bear markets. In a bull market, their role is to deliver competitive returns consistent with your tolerance for risk. In bear markets, their role is to help you lose less than the markets and protect your principal. Over both market cycles, their role is to achieve your goals. Advisors should be entrusted with your financial future only when they can perform in both types of markets.

Trust Must Be Earned

In an ideal world, your initial trust in an advisor is based on objective selection criteria that you control. However, real trust comes only with time and measurable results. At the end of each calendar year, your annual review process should include a determination about the competence and trustworthiness of your current financial professional.

SUMMARY

✔ The financial services industry has a history of questionable business practices. To this day, it fights to avoid investor-friendly regulations, such as full disclosure.

✔ Personal financial advisors are the distribution system for the industry. Their role is to generate revenue for the industry's companies and produce income for themselves.

✔ The majority of advisors are not trustworthy because they put their needs and the needs of their companies ahead of yours.

✔ The industry knows that money moves on trust, so it has taught advisors to build relationships on self-professed trust that is used to gain your confidence.

✔ Once advisors have won your trust and assets, they are free to sell whatever generates the most income and revenue for themselves and their companies.

✔ You can avoid being the victim by learning how to select competent, trustworthy advisors.

✔ Trust must be based on measurable knowledge and integrity. There is no other way for you to protect your financial future.

3

SERVICE PROVIDERS

The financial services industry is frequently criticized for deliberately making relatively simple information and processes more complex than they have to be. This is no doubt a carryover from years past, when investors were totally dependent on Wall Street for investment information, advice, and execution. Unnecessary complexity within the industry increases investor dependency on its services, making them easier to market.

What can be confusing for many investors is that a number of service providers are needed to generate a comprehensive investment solution. Each company, division, or professional provides a specialized service and charges a separate fee, one layered on top of another. In addition to providers across categories, there can also be multiple providers within the same service category. Take money managers, for example. It is typical to have an IRA with not one, but four or five money managers, and for good reason: you want multiple managers for diversification that reduces overall risk. There are also services for which only one provider makes sense. Your financial consultant, tax advisor, attorney, and custodian are good examples of this.

This chapter describes the roles of various providers and why you need them to arrive at a comprehensive solution for your assets.

The Ultimate Decision Maker

When it comes to your assets, you retain all of the responsibilities which you choose not to delegate to professionals. For example, you could research and select money managers, in which case you would be acting as your own advisor and decision maker. An alternative would be to delegate the research to an advisor but still retain control over the decision making. This is the most frequent relationship between investors and advisors. You could also delegate both by giving the professional the research and decision making authority, or discretion, over your assets. However, even in this last scenario, you are still the ultimate decision maker, because only you have the power to hire and fire the advisor—the proverbial buck inevitably stops with you. This may be your only role in the investment process, because it cannot be delegated. Professionals can perform all other work on your behalf.

The Personal Financial Advisor

The most important service provider you will ever hire is a personal financial advisor because this individual has more influence or control over the investment of your assets than any other professional. Some advisors deliver a number of high-value services that provide the structure and process for investing your assets in the securities markets.

Three Types of Advisors

There are several types of advisors that are distinguished by their services, licenses, credentials, and methods of compensation. To make their differentiation easier to understand, I have consolidated them into three primary categories: consultants, planners, and financial representatives. All three are referred to as advisors throughout the book, and a chapter is dedicated to each with a comprehensive service description.

Be aware that advisors have various roles, and there is a huge range in quality among them. In addition, there are no regulations that govern the titles or roles that advisors can assume. For example, insurance agents frequently call themselves planners, even though they may have limited planning expertise.

One Personal Financial Advisor

You may believe that having multiple advisors is a form of diversification that will reduce your overall risk. This is the foundation of a number of problems which you can avoid with one quality professional. Multiple advisors actually reduce performance, while increasing risk and expense. For example, assume that you invest your assets through two advisors who each recommend overlapping strategies (a reasonable outcome because they were both looking at the same profile data). You have just increased your expense and risk.

Most investors allocate assets to multiple advisors because they do not trust any one professional with all of their money. They feel safer when their assets are divided among several companies and advisors. This is a false sense of security. The real key to your financial future is to hire one very competent advisor whom you can trust, then make that professional responsible for diversifying your assets among several high-quality money managers. This way, you maximize performance while minimizing risk and expense.

Advisor As Coordinator

If you are a typical investor, you will have little or no time to be involved in the numerous details that will make your financial goals a reality. Consequently, you want a service provider who can act as the coordinator for the other professionals and companies that provide services for your assets. The provider capable of acting as the coordinator is your personal financial advisor.

You should make this advisor your initial hire and assign him or her the task of helping you select the rest of the professionals on your team—for example, the custodian, money managers, and the financial planner. Once the team is selected, it is the advisor's role to act as the coordinator. Keep in mind that if you do not delegate the role of coordinator, you will have to assume the responsibilities by default. The only other alternative is to not have a coordinator, in which case your assets are exposed to additional risk, expense, and potential perform-ance problems.

The optimal type of advisor/coordinator is the consultant, because this professional's singular focus is the investment and performance of your assets. Advisors who focus on the planning process generally do not provide the same level of investment advice, although some have both skills. You do not want a financial representative as your coor-dinator, because they are sales professionals and do not have ongoing sources of compensation that cover the costs of the continuous coor-dination services.

The Advisor As Gatekeeper

A quality advisor can also act as the gatekeeper for your financial interests, meaning that all other potential service and product providers have to go through that professional to get to you. The advisor screens out the bad ideas, products, services, and profession-als and only presents those that are consistent with your philosophy, needs, goals, and tolerance for risk. This valuable service helps you avoid bad products that are marketed by skilled professionals with finely honed (but frequently deceptive) sales presentations. They may be able to fool you, but they should not be able to fool your advi-sor/gatekeeper. A quality advisor is the perfect gatekeeper for your interests, because this professional will know you and your financial needs better than anyone else.

The Financial Consultant

Every individual should have a financial consultant to help invest assets in the securities markets. This highly skilled specialist has the ability to help you perform a number of critical tasks that must be accomplished if you wish to achieve your goals. For example, the con-sultant will help you develop an investment strategy, allocate assets, select money managers, and report performance each quarter. These are high-value services when provided by a competent, trustworthy professional. Due to the strategic nature of their services, a consult-ant is also the ideal coordinator and gatekeeper for your financial future, because other professionals may provide specialized services that impact your assets, but none have the direct impact of a consultant on the investment of those assets.

Consultants are described in more detail in Chapter Seven.

The Financial Planner

You also need the services of a financial planner who can take a complete view of your current situation and recommend a strategy for achieving lifetime goals. This is much different from the consultant who only recommends strategies for the investment of your assets. The planner helps you determine, for example, how much you should be saving versus how much you can safely spend on your lifestyle. He or she also helps you calculate how much is needed for your children's education or your retirement. The discipline of a quality plan should be an integral part of your financial strategy.

Think of your financial plan as a roadmap in life. There are stops along the way, such as your children's education, major purchases, and financial emergencies. Your ultimate "destination" is a comfortable retirement. Unused assets will become part of your estate to be dispersed according to your will. A quality financial plan will help you maximize the probability of achieving all of these goals.

Planner/Consultant

A very small percentage of high-quality planners also have the specialized knowledge to be your consultant. They help you develop a financial plan; then they help you implement it by recommending particular investments. A much larger percentage of planners do not have consulting skills and simply sell you products that maximize their incomes. Keep in mind that even if they tell you they have consulting skills or call themselves consultants, it could just be "spin" designed to help them win your trust and assets.

Planners are described in more detail in Chapter Eight.

The Financial Representative

The financial representative is the least skilled advisor because this professional does not have the specialized knowledge of the consultant or the planner. They typically hold licenses that only permit the sale of financial products, such as mutual funds and annuities. Instead of providing advice that is knowledge-based, their recommendations are part of the sales process they use to win your assets. Their advice is frequently tainted by low-quality recommendations that benefit the representatives or their companies more than you.

Due to their general lack of competence and trustworthiness, financial representatives should be your last choice as an advisor. You may lack choices because you do not have enough assets to obtain the services of a higher skilled advisor. Your only alternatives may be to act as your own advisor or select a financial representative.

The Money Manager

Money managers are the decision makers for the securities (stocks and bonds) in your portfolio. Most money managers are specialists, so you will need one for each asset class and style of management, such as large capitalization (asset class) growth (style) stocks. However, there are also managers who are generalists and invest in multiple asset classes. The best example of a generalist is a balanced manager that invests in both stocks and bonds. Managers are also differentiated by the geographic sector in which they invest—domestic, international, or global.

You need money managers because they have the knowledge to invest your assets in the securities markets. Advisors do not have these skills. Consequently, one of the primary responsibilities of advisors is to help you select quality managers for your assets. The main responsibility of the managers is to build and maintain a portfolio of securities based on your requirements and their investment outlooks, philosophies, and research.

Diversified Manager Strategy

Too many investors believe they are diversifying their investment strategy when they hire multiple advisors. As pointed out in other sections of this book, this is a flawed strategy. There is only one way to diversify your assets and that is by hiring multiple managers over various asset classes. Why? Because it is nearly impossible to identify with 100% certainty the asset class that will perform the best (or more importantly, the worst). You are better off diversifying among quality managers.

Active Versus Passive Managers

There are several references in this book to active and passive managers. There is a simple explanation for the differences between the two. Think of active managers as trying to "beat" the performance of something—a benchmark or peers are common goals. Think of passive managers as trying to "match" the performance of something—almost always an index.

Active managers take more risk than passive managers because of their need to outperform benchmarks or peers. For example, you invest with a particular manager because the company has a history of outperforming the S&P 500, an index of 500 large U.S. companies. The manager takes more risk than the S&P 500 because it is trying to beat the performance of the index. The manager also charges a higher fee because professionals who try to beat the market are more expensive than professionals who are trying to match the market. As you might imagine, the higher fees and risk are supposed to be offset by higher performance.

On the other hand, passive managers are trying to match the performance of the S&P 500 within a few tenths of percent. For example, if the index is up ten percent the passive manager should be up 9.8 percent to 10.2 percent. This is a less expensive investment process than active management so the fees are lower, usually much lower. You are also not taking the risk of active management, trying to beat the index, so your exposure to the risks of investing in securities is lower.

Some investors use all active managers, some use all passive managers, and many use a blend of the two.

Specialists and Generalists

The industry would like you to believe that money managers are only good at working with one asset class, style of management, or geography. However, this is not true. Managers with quality investment processes and professionals can work with multiple classes, styles, and geographies. This is evidenced by the fact that most managers of large asset amounts offer multiple products. Think of a mutual fund company with 200 funds or a separate account manager with five products. Class, style, geography, and other variables differentiate the products.

You should invest in multiple asset classes, styles of management, and geographies to minimize your risk. However, this does not mean that you need a large number of managers. This is especially true if you have smaller asset amounts and want to invest with separate account managers. For example, you could select a global, balanced, core manager who would invest your assets in several classes, styles, and geographies. This is a simpler and more cost-effective solution than using several managers, although it is frequently difficult to find managers who excel in all categories.

Separate Account Managers

One of the two primary types of managers is a *separate account manager*. When investing through this type of manager, your assets are not commingled with the assets of any other investor—hence the name "separate account." Having your own portfolio produces several important benefits:

- Your performance is not impacted by cash flows of other investors.
- The portfolio can be tailored to your personal tastes. For example, you may want to exclude tobacco, alcohol, gambling, or nuclear stocks from your portfolio.
- This type of management can be less expensive than pooled management.
- It is easier to manage risk when your assets are in separate accounts.
- Your portfolio can be managed for higher levels of tax efficiency.

Pooled Managers

The other popular type of management is referred to as *pooled*, which means that your assets are commingled with those of other investors. There are several popular types of pooled management investments, including mutual funds, exchange traded funds, hedge funds, and trust funds. Pooled managers also provide specific benefits to investors:

- They provide professional management for smaller asset amounts.
- It is easier to diversify smaller amounts of assets when using pooled management.

The Insurance Specialist

Most financial professionals will volunteer to be your insurance advisor to satisfy your need for insurance products. Do not let this offer mislead you. The motivation for this offer, for too many advisors, is the opportunity to earn large commissions. This is definitely a double-edged sword. There is no question that you need insurance products to protect your family, income, and assets. But should a financial advisor also be your insurance advisor? Or do you require a specialist?

Insurance Products

Insurance products, like investment products, can be extremely complicated due to their quantity, the differences between products, and the deliberate obfuscation by the insurance industry. There are annuities, various forms of life insurance, casualty insurance, health insurance, long-term care insurance, and many others. You need an insurance specialist whose primary responsibility is to provide adequate protection for a reasonable price—not to sell unnecessary products or large policies just to maximize commissions. The latter frequently occurs, though, when advisors with existing relationships abuse your trust by selling unnecessary amounts of coverage.

Insurance Agent/Planner

A high percentage of planners are former insurance agents. In most cases, they offer relatively unsophisticated services and make most of their money implementing the "recommendations" of their plans. The title change from agent to planner was designed to eliminate the stigma of being called an insurance agent. Remember, titles may have nothing to do with actual duties or core competence. In this case, it was primarily a sales ploy.

Insurance Agent/Representative

An equally high percentage of insurance advisors are also licensed to market investment products like mutual funds and variable annuities. The critical question for you to ask is whether the advisor is highly skilled in both investment and insurance products—it may be one, the other, or both. The most frequent answer is no, in which case you have exposed your assets to unnecessary risk.

Insurance Agent/Consultant

It is rare for an insurance professional to also have asset consulting skills. Asset consulting is the most sophisticated of the investment services and generally requires a specialized professional. You do not want a professional who is a strong insurance specialist and a weak financial consultant providing both services.

The Custodian

Investors worry unnecessarily about advisors or managers absconding with their assets. Their concerns appear justified when they read the large number of financial horror stories in their local newspapers. However, the stories are rarely about securities, which have built-in protections. They are usually about mortgage investments gone awry: an individual writes a check to the provider but the funds are never invested. There is no question that investment scams are a reality. But the safety of your physical assets should not be a major concern when you invest in the securities markets. Your first line of defense is a quality custodian.

Possession of assets is the primary role of the custodian, which is usually a clearing broker/dealer like Merrill Lynch, Smith Barney, Wells Fargo Securities, Charles Schwab, Fidelity's National Financial Services, Bank of New York's Pershing, or TD Waterhouse. Banks with trust departments also provide custodial services. You should always make sure that your assets are held by a reputable firm in order to minimize any concerns about physical safety. Your minimum criteria for a firm should be that it is a member of the Securities Investor Protection Corporation (SIPC), maintains a large commercial insurance policy for your protection, is responsible for billions of dollars, and has been in business more than ten years.

Advisors and managers should never have direct contact with your assets, either when you initially invest or down the road. If you fund your account with a check instead of an asset transfer, always make it payable to the custodian. Advisors and managers should only have access to the fees that they charge for their services.

To minimize the impact of this perceived risk, many investors will custody assets at multiple locations, primarily banks and brokerage firms. This is based on the same logic as hiring multiple advisors—investors think that bad things can only happen to a portion of their assets. But there is no practical reason to place your assets with multiple custodians. In fact, this strategy only muddies the water and makes the coordination, monitoring, and reporting processes for your assets more difficult and more expensive.

One-Stop Shopping

Your advisor may be an employee of your custodian. For example, your advisor may work for Merrill Lynch and the custodian may be a Merrill Lynch company. There is nothing wrong with this relationship, particularly if the company in question is well-known and delivers a high level of service for a competitive overall fee.

The Trustee

Individuals and firms use the trust services of banks and independent trust companies for a variety of services. For example, a couple might hire a bank to be the trustee of their children's trust or a business might hire a trustee to oversee its qualified retirement plan. In both examples, the couple and the business are moving fiduciary (legal) responsibility for asset decisions from themselves to the corporate trustee.

Trust Services

There are two primary types of corporate trustees: bank trust departments and independent trust companies. You can also act as your own trustee, as can nonprofit institutions. Both categories of corporate trustees deliver the same services, although many trustees choose to specialize in particular types of assets, such as personal or pension. Following are the important services offered by trust departments and companies for individual assets:

- Trustee
- Custodial
- Asset management

- Executor
- Tax and investment reporting
- Personal trust

Trust Features

One of the advantages of turning your assets over to a trust entity is succession. For example, assume that you are your own trustee, but suffer a stroke and are no longer able to manage your own financial affairs. If you have a legal document that names a bank as your successor trustee, it takes over the management of your financial affairs including paying bills and managing real estate.

If you were unfortunate enough to meet a premature demise leaving minor children, a trust established in your will would authorize a trustee to act as the decision maker for your assets. This also leads to another trust advantage—perpetuity. Whereas people die or become disabled, trustees are corporations that can last forever. Therefore, you do not have to worry about the availability of trust services years into the future.

The Tax Advisor

Your goal should be to minimize the amount of tax you pay the government for investing your assets. This requires a strategy that is part of the investment process and is implemented through your financial advisor. At the same time, tax strategies for your financial investments are part of a much bigger picture that includes nonfinancial assets. For example, you may have taxable gains from the sale of real estate investments that you would like to offset with taxable losses from securities investments—or vice versa. Now you have entered the territory of the certified public accountant (CPA) who, like your planner, has a more complete view of your assets and financial situation. It is the role of the CPA to help you minimize your overall taxes during all phases of your financial life, including those related to your estate.

The Tax and Financial Advisor

Thousands of CPAs are entering the financial services industry to leverage their existing relationships with you. In fact, the American Institute of Certified Public Accountants estimates that 35 percent of its members will eventually provide some combination of tax and financial advice.

Most CPA firms have adopted a planning model for their financial service businesses. They provide tax and financial planning separately or in a package for a single fee. This is an important service combination, because there are numerous tax issues in financial plans. A much smaller percentage of CPAs have adopted the consulting model, because it requires a higher level of investment knowledge that is foreign to most tax professionals.

Instead of one person playing the roles of both the tax and financial advisor, some accounting firms have staffed planning and investment departments with experienced professionals to deliver these services as part of a team of specialists. This way, the respective advisors can focus on their specialties. Other firms have entered into marketing relationships with third parties to provide the financial, non-tax services. In the latter case, the CPA firm receives a referral fee for recommending the services of their strategic partner.

Tax Planning Services

Tax planning is a high-value service that should be coordinated with your advisor's financial advice. Depending upon your income and assets, the planning process may be relatively simple or extraordinarily complex. Your tax professional's first responsibility is to make sure you never pay more taxes than necessary. This includes taxes on income, rents, royalties, dividends, interest, and capital gains. To accomplish this goal, your tax and financial advisors must work together.

Tax-Based Investment Strategies

Your most prominent financial goal should be to maximize your returns consistent with your tolerance for risk. However, your real objective is more complex: it is to maximize net returns, in particular, net of taxes, inflation, and fees you pay for financial services. Unless your assets are in an IRA or qualified retirement plan, they can be eroded by taxes on capital gains, dividends, and interest.

Your investment strategy should therefore be influenced by your tax situation. For example, investments producing significant income streams should be held in your IRAs where they can accumulate tax-deferred. For the same reason, investments that appreciate substantially should be held in taxable accounts to take advantage of lower capital gains taxes. What you sell and when you sell should be influenced, but not controlled, by tax considerations. Whether you own municipal or corporate bonds is a tax-related issue that impacts net returns.

The Legal Professional

Your team should also include legal professionals who have very important responsibilities in regard to your assets. You may use a living trust to hold title to your assets and avoid probate, the process of legally establishing the validity of a will. You also may have estate plans and wills to protect your heirs and govern the disposition of your assets. The legal professional's responsibilities can overlap with those of your tax advisor. For example, your estate plan should be designed to minimize the amount of tax you pay while maximizing the amount of assets you bequeath to your heirs and charity.

A comprehensive investment strategy should always be coordinated with your attorney to ensure that your assets and financial goals are accurately reflected in legal documents. You must make sure that all of your accounts are held in the appropriate name(s) and that the names of the beneficiaries of the accounts are accurate. Also, what happens to minor children in the unlikely event of the premature death of both spouses? Who has control over your assets and how income is disbursed are extremely important questions to be addressed when your goal is to protect the interests of your children.

The Team of Experts

In the near future, you will find an increasing number of asset service providers offering you combinations of services from the same firm. This level of service should have occurred years ago, but several laws and regulations forced companies to limit their service offerings.

For example, in the not-so-distant past:

- Banks could offer only banking services.
- CPAs could offer only tax and audit services.
- Brokerage firms could market only financial products and trade securities.

- Attorneys could provide only legal services.
- Agents could sell only insurance products.

Most of the laws that created this separation were established in the post-Depression 1930s and 40s when politicians passed regulations to protect the public from industries that impacted the financial security of individuals. Powerful lobbyists from the insurance, banking, and brokerage industries also influenced politicians to pass restrictive legislation designed to protect their franchises from new competitors. Fortunately, most of these restrictive laws and practices were rescinded in the late twentieth century. However, the new freedom for companies to enter each other's businesses creates new risks for your financial future, in particular the competence of new types of companies and advisors who are entering the financial services industry.

Advisor Combinations

Several combinations of service providers will be available to you in the future based upon your needs. The core services are financial, tax, and legal advice; however there are also:

- Banking services
- Mortgage services
- Insurance services

The Leveraged Relationship

The motivation of many of these new entrants into the financial services industry is to leverage an existing relationship with you. For example, your banker, CPA, and insurance agent would also like to be advising you financially in order to build upon trust that has already been established. By doing this, they can generate additional revenue streams. The new revenue stream is usually very profitable, because the costs associated with new client acquisition are low when they cross-sell additional services to existing relationships.

There is nothing wrong with leveraging relationships, as long as each service is of high quality and the services increase efficiency and lower overall expense to you. Your challenge is to determine the quality of each service. Never forget that the companies entered the financial services industry to increase their revenue and profits, not to help you do a better job with your assets.

The Benefits of Teams

Professional teams can provide substantial benefits to investors who have enough assets to attract their services. These benefits include the following:

- Efficiency of a completely coordinated solution for your assets
- Convenience of one-stop shopping
- Reduced expenses because the professionals share common information that does not have to be reproduced by each provider
- Substantial time savings
- Asset-based fees can pay for multiple services

When specialized professionals work in teams, there a is greater likelihood that you will achieve your financial goals. For example, your investment strategy will reflect the goals in your financial plan, you will pay fewer taxes, and your legal documents will reflect your financial goals. Technology will also reduce your expenses. Once your profile and account information are in the database, multiple professionals can utilize it instead of each one charging you to enter the information separately.

The Multi-Family Office

Very wealthy families have used the family office concept for years. They have complex needs and require coordinated services to achieve their goals. A new version of this service is the multi-family office that is staffed by professionals who work with multiple high net worth families.

Services provided by the multi-family office include: lifestyle issues that include where and how to live, a number of planning services, diversification strategies, risk management, philanthropy, financial education, and family continuity. Some offices also include integrated tax and legal advice. This level of service is highly desirable, and enterprising advisors will find a way to make it available to investors with smaller amounts of assets.

SUMMARY

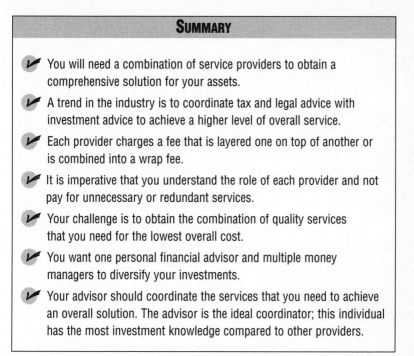

✔ You will need a combination of service providers to obtain a comprehensive solution for your assets.

✔ A trend in the industry is to coordinate tax and legal advice with investment advice to achieve a higher level of overall service.

✔ Each provider charges a fee that is layered one on top of another or is combined into a wrap fee.

✔ It is imperative that you understand the role of each provider and not pay for unnecessary or redundant services.

✔ Your challenge is to obtain the combination of quality services that you need for the lowest overall cost.

✔ You want one personal financial advisor and multiple money managers to diversify your investments.

✔ Your advisor should coordinate the services that you need to achieve an overall solution. The advisor is the ideal coordinator; this individual has the most investment knowledge compared to other providers.

4

CONFLICTS OF INTEREST

The financial services industry suffers from numerous conflicts of interest for two primary reasons. First, its foundation is based on a culture that rewards advisors for the sale of financial products rather than the achievement of your financial goals. Second, it is standard industry practice to put the interests of shareholders, key company employees, and financial advisors ahead of investors' interests. For example, we all know about the seven- and eight-figure bonuses that are paid to key executives, research analysts, and "big producers." Too often, these bonuses are achieved at your expense.

According to Lewis Braham in *Business Week Online*, if the medical profession were as loosely defined as the financial advice business, witch doctors would share the same page in the phone book as brain surgeons. Almost anyone can claim to be a financial planner or investment advisor and there are a myriad of credentials an advisor can appropriate—some are familiar while others are obscure.

It stands to reason that the industry can make more money when it places its personal and business interests ahead of yours. One of the most frequent examples of this is when you are sold a lower-quality product that pays higher revenues to companies and increased commissions to advisors. It happens every day, and no laws are being broken. Naïve investors simply trust the wrong advisors with their assets. The bottom line is that we live in a world of *caveat emptor*—let the buyer beware. It is therefore up to us to learn to protect our own financial interests. The regulators are not going to do it for us, nor will the financial services industry or most of its advisors. We must learn to recognize these conflicts ourselves in order to avoid them.

Conflicts Are Reality

Financial advisors, like most people, are striving to make the best livings possible for themselves and their families. The principal difference between financial advisors and other types of professionals is that they make their livings by generating income from your assets—the same assets you depend on to achieve your financial goals. When these interests collide, you are always the loser.

Reality

You are accumulating or preserving assets that will produce income for a secure, comfortable retirement. In a perfect world, you would maximize the net return on your assets, advisors would maximize personal incomes, and companies would maximize revenues and profits when you achieve your goals. In the real world, however, all of these interests compete with one another. You lose because, believe it or not, advisors control their relationship with you. It may not be obvious, but it is very real.

Michael Collins on CBS *Market Watch* reported that Andre Pineda said that the only person that an individual investor can be sure does not have some conflict of interest is the individual investor. Trust yourself, and get independent confirmation of any advice you are getting, Pineda said. The fact that you are getting advice from the biggest names in the business does not necessarily mean you are getting good advice.

Lack of Disclosure

Ideally, professionals would volunteer all of the information you need to make a quality decision for your financial future. The disclosures would include credentials, conflicts of interest, and compensation. However, this rarely happens; in fact, the industry spends hundreds of millions of dollars per year on lobbyists to avoid disclosure. You might wonder why there is not more disclosure in the industry. The answer is simple: a high percentage of advisors are incompetent and conflicts of interest are a way of doing business. Full disclosure would compromise the industry's ability to put weak advisors into the field quickly and to sell mediocre products. The sad truth is that withholding important data improves the bottom lines of the industry's companies.

Winning the Sale

The advisors' need to win your assets motivates the withholding of information. Many professionals will do whatever is necessary to win, because they have everything to gain and nothing to lose. You know now that these advisors will not volunteer any facts that are detrimental to their personal interests, so you must learn to ask the right questions. Otherwise, you risk turning your assets over to the wrong professional.

Paul Farrell on CBS *Market Watch* reported that most investors are living in fantasyland, believing their broker "was looking out for their interests first." This is a very dangerous assumption. Two thirds of all mutual funds are sold by commissioned brokers, who are salespeople, not advisors. They make a living selling things, whether you need them or not. And they'll tell you anything to get you to buy. Test this by asking commissioned brokers to recommend an alternative no-load fund that is just as good as the load fund they are selling you. Watch the broker's eyes glaze over!

Conflicted Information

If you are like most investors, you will gather a certain amount of information from advisors before you select one. Once the selection is made, it may be years before you realize that you have made a mistake. The use of hindsight, usually provoked by poor performance, allows you to know that you have an inferior advisor. However, people rarely connect the quality problem to the information they were given when they made the selection decision. Information that is incomplete or inaccurate is very difficult to identify, evaluate, and record—especially if it is verbal. This is why so many people select incompetent, untrustworthy advisors; they sound great when they present the reasons why you should hire them.

However, if you did have "complete and accurate" information on a particular advisor, you probably would never select that individual in the first place. By the time you know this, though, it is always too late. It is not possible to go back and recover the lost years and the lost performance.

Investment Information

We have all read about the decades of conflicted research done by Wall Street to maximize its investment banking revenues and other income streams from companies they report on. This is just one example of the trustworthiness of advice that is dispensed by Wall Street and its advisors. Another example is asset allocation. Industry strategists recommend frequent changes in allocation based on their forecasts of future market conditions. In the not-too-distant past, frequent change meant substantial revenues for companies and their advisors. Millions of transactions were processed every time a highly regarded "strategist" recommended increasing or decreasing your allocation to stocks. The more changes you made to your portfolio by following their advice, the more money the firms and their advisors made.

Misrepresentation

Misrepresentation of information is one of the most common abuses practiced by many advisors. It occurs in sales and service processes because so much information is communicated verbally, making it easy to deny later. The opportunities to misrepresent information are only limited by the imagination and ethics of the advisor. Your only protection is to require all important information in writing so that you have a permanent record of it.

As an example, assume that an advisor works in an office with nine other professionals, and you ask the advisor the amount of fee-based assets he or she handles. The answer is $300 million. The number impresses you enough to select the professional as your advisor. However, because the asset amount was for all ten advisors—not just the advisor you were interviewing—there is misrepresentation. The reason behind the misrepresentation is that the advisor you interviewed was new and controlled less than $2 million. The professional did not believe it was possible to win your assets with an accurate response to your question. If the facts surfaced later, the advisor could simply say that he or she thought your question was in regard to the amount of assets serviced by the entire office, not just him or her.

Omission

Sometimes it is not what the advisors say; it is what they do not say. I think this practice is even more prevalent than misrepresentation, because it is very difficult to prove that you were damaged by information that was deliberately withheld. It is not the fault of the professional that you did not know enough to ask the right questions. In addition, there is no law that requires advisors to volunteer sensitive information that may cost them the sale.

This is also a better strategy when dealing with industry regulators who have never mandated full disclosure, or for that matter, any type of real disclosure by advisors who are not Registered Investment Advisors (RIAs). For example, let us say that an advisor you are interviewing has only one year of experience in the financial services industry. The advisor will never volunteer this information to you, because you would more than likely use it as a reason to exclude this professional from your selection process. Once again, the advisor has everything to gain and nothing to lose by not providing the information. If the advisor's lack of experience negatively impacts the performance of your assets, it is your problem—you failed to ask the right questions during the interview.

Deliberate Obscurity

Another tactic that creates conflict is deliberate obscurity. Information is provided, but it is buried in technical jargon that means little or nothing to you. The documents that advisors use to sign you up as a client are classic examples of this. They are designed to be difficult to understand; consequently, most investors do not read them, and the industry knows that. If you knew what you were really buying, you might not buy it. This is not in the industry's best interests.

Advisor Compensation

Nowhere is the potential for conflict of interest greater than in the compensation of advisors. That is because virtually all advisors have significant discretion when it comes to recommending particular investments for your assets. They can sell you higher- or lower-quality products that pay varying amounts of compensation—a major conflict. This is the number one reason why you want a fee-based advisor. They should make the same amount of money regardless of what they recommend for investment.

Third Party Compensation

You have two choices when it comes to compensating advisors: you can pay them fees, or a third party can pay them using various forms of commissions. When third parties pay professionals to provide services for your assets, you have to question whom the advisors work for—you or the third party? Since most people work for their source of compensation, you have to assume that there is an inherent conflict of interest when a third party pays for professional advice that will impact your one and only financial future.

Time Versus Compensation

At the core of the compensation conflict is the advisor's ability to spend a few hours with you and earn thousands of dollars of compensation from the sale of investment products. This is the principal reason why commission professionals do not want you to know their compensation amounts. Most often, there is no relationship between compensation and time. Advisors also know that you would be very surprised, and most likely upset, if you knew the amount of money that they earned from your assets. Their strategy is not to bring it up and hope that you do not, either.

Compensation Versus Value

If you are going to pay an advisor thousands of dollars of compensation, you should expect to receive substantial value in return. This is a conflict, because most advisors do not have the knowledge gained from education and experience to provide high added value—they are merely sales representatives. The value you are looking for is the strategy that will provide the highest probability of achieving your financial goals for the least amount of risk and expense.

Compensation Versus Results

Commission advisors are paid within thirty days of the sale. The quick payment of commissions—some are as frequent as weekly—is the immediate financial reward that these types of professionals and their companies are seeking. It also means that they have no downside if their products fail to meet your expectations; they were paid months or years ago. A professional's compensation should always be impacted by the results of his or her advice.

You Pay Commissions Anyway

Commission advisors would like you to believe that their services are free because third parties pay them. This statement is simply not true. There are no free lunches in the financial services industry. Ultimately, you pay all overhead and profit margins for the products and services you use. Therefore, commissions are part of the expense structure of the product provider, which you pay with management and administration fees. For example, a front-end load is a commission that is deducted from your assets, and a back-end load is a commission that is paid up front to the advisor. It is recovered by charging you higher expenses for the product. You pay all commissions, but you have no control over the ongoing service or amount of compensation. Control is not a problem, however, when you pay a fee for services.

High-Expense Products

Financial products, such as mutual funds, annuities, and life insurance have various expense structures which range from reasonable to inexcusably high. The higher expenses are rarely justified by superior returns. More often, they reflect the cost structures of the products and the profit requirements of the companies. The number one expense of any product, at least initially, is the compensation that is paid to advisors for selling the products to you.

It is relatively easy for advisors to market expensive products to less knowledgeable investors. They only show higher-cost products and do not offer less expensive alternatives. Less experienced investors wrongfully assume that all products have the same higher expense ratios. The advisor bets that you will not know that the fees and commissions are excessive. If you buy the products, you've lost the bet. The advisor collects substantial compensation for very little work.

Commission Rates

One interesting characteristic of the financial services industry is the range of advisor compensation that is available for selling similar products. Two mutual funds with the same track record can have substantially different expense ratios. The compensation to advisors can also vary, which tests their integrity. The conflict is clear: do they sell the best product for you or the product with the largest amount of compensation for them?

Objectivity and Compensation

The objective advice you expect from advisors can evaporate if the compensation is high enough. This is what happened to Wall Street in the 1990s. The companies were taking in enormous short-term profits and paying their professionals substantial amounts of compensation. The urge to sell the latest hot investment was out of control. The frenzy caused all objectivity to go out the window and greed took its place.

Meeting Quotas

Quotas are a fact of life in the financial services industry. This is because a major brokerage firm's cost of supporting an advisor can be well in excess of $100,000 per year. As a result, these companies put significant pressure on advisors to produce enough revenue to cover personal expenses, support costs, general overhead, and profit margins.

Advisors can also be Independent Contractors (ICs) who may be licensed with broker/dealers. Whereas companies pay the expenses of employees, ICs pay their own expenses. Consequently they have to generate enough revenue to cover their costs and produce income to live on. Their need is not a quota, but it has the same net effect.

Keeping Their Jobs

If advisors' number one goal is personal income, then their second goal is to keep their jobs by producing sufficient revenue to cover all company or personal costs and produce a profit—the money generated by meeting the quota. The advisors' need to achieve specific revenue goals can be in conflict with your interests.

- They may have quotas for particular products.
- They may sell lower-quality products that produce higher revenues.
- They may promote particular products simply to meet month-end quota requirements.
- They may sell you commission products rather than fee-based services to produce more immediate revenue.
- They may sell products that benefit their companies instead of you.
- They may churn your accounts (unnecessary buying and selling) to generate additional revenues.

Nothing motivates an individual quite as much as the fear of job loss and not being able to pay the bills. You want to be very sure that your advisor is not struggling to stay employed.

Money, Recognition, and Awards

In addition to quotas, financial service companies have developed a number of other strategies for motivating advisors to sell more products and gather more assets from clients. Money, recognition, and awards are the common incentives.

The imbedded conflict is that none of these strategies recognize or reward advisors for competent advice. In fact, most financial service companies do not even know how to measure competency in relation to the achievement of investor goals. As management guru Peter Drucker says, "If you can't measure it, you can't manage it."

Assets and revenues are easy for companies to measure, and they both contribute to profits—their ultimate goal. Whenever the principal motivation of advisors is limited to controlling assets that produce revenues, it is inevitable that this goal will take precedence over your needs—a major conflict.

Asset Amounts

Most fee-based advisors prefer to work with larger asset amounts. A one percent fee on smaller asset amounts does not generate sufficient revenue to cover the professional's costs and produce a profit. For this reason, investors with larger asset amounts receive higher levels of service than those with lower amounts.

Level of Service

A major conflict of interest occurs when you do not receive the level of service that you deserve based on the revenue you generate for advisors. Some professionals may shortchange you, because the less time they spend servicing, the more time they can spend selling products and capturing new assets. Most advisors make more money selling than they do providing the services that they promised during the sales process. The reason for this is that the fee participation or commission rate is higher for new sales than it is for ongoing servicing.

Smaller Asset Amounts

Investors with smaller asset amounts—less than $100,000 and perhaps even as much as $250,000—are subject to a much higher risk of bad advice. They do not have sufficient assets to hire better-quality professionals. An advisor charging a one percent fee on an investment of $50,000 would make $500 per year of annual compensation. This conflict negatively impacts smaller investors; their only option for a financial advisor may be a representative who sells investment products for commissions.

Investment Products

When it comes to financial products, you already know that there are great ones, terrible ones, and everything in between. Great products are well managed, have competitive track records, and charge reasonable expenses. Terrible products have weak management, poor results, and charge outrageous expenses. As a result, all investment professionals are tested every time they recommend a product because they have to make a choice on quality versus personal income. This is why integrity is the most important advisor characteristic. In the final analysis, you have to learn to recognize bad advice and bad products to protect your financial future.

Product Quality

Lower-quality investment products frequently compete for distribution by offering higher payouts to advisors. The product company is hoping that the advisors will overlook product deficiencies, which hurt investors, in order to earn higher incomes for themselves. As you might imagine, this strategy appeals to many advisors—those who are willing to put their interests ahead of yours.

Professionals have various techniques for convincing you to buy low-quality products:

- They build a relationship of trust and then violate it by selling low-quality, high-payout products.
- They show you multiple products, so you think that you have a choice. All the products, however, are low-quality alternatives.
- They do not disclose the shortcomings of the low-quality products to you. It is up to you to know the qualitative differences.

Proprietary Investment Products

The company that employs or contracts the services of the advisor may produce its own products including mutual funds, annuities, life insurance, separate account management services, and limited partnerships. Companies and their advisors may push these products because they produce higher profit margins for the companies and higher monetary incentives for the advisors. This process is a major conflict of interest when the product is inferior to other choices in terms of performance, risk, and expense.

For example, let us say that Bob Smith, an advisor for Acme Financial Services, only recommends mutual funds from the Acme Family of Funds. He tells you that this is the best fund family in America and that is why he is recommending it. What he omitted from his presentation, however, was the fact that there are hundreds of other funds with better management, better track records, reduced risk characteristics, and lower expense ratios. It is Acme's policy, though, that Bob recommend the company's funds for all or part of your assets, or he will be terminated.

It is also important to note that many proprietary products are competitive with products provided by third parties. In some cases, they represent very high-quality products. You must determine the quality before investing in the product. Excessive use of proprietary products by advisors is highly undesirable for the investor.

Third Party Products

The practice of limiting your choices also occurs with third party products, and it represents the same conflict of interest. However, because third party products have the appearance of choice (you are not limited to proprietary products), the strategy of limiting choices is more difficult to identify and avoid.

Just as they do with proprietary products, financial services companies may limit your choices to particular third party products because they earn substantial amounts of money to recommend certain products. They are paid upfront fees or share in the revenues of the product providers. This is pure profit for the financial services companies and is rarely, if ever, disclosed to investors. The products are recommended not because they are the best investment for you, but because the company receives additional compensation to recommend them. There is no disclosure for this practice, and it is a major conflict of interest.

Red Flags

Conflicts of interest exhibit frequent warning signs for knowledgeable investors who know what to watch for. I call these signs *red flags*, and they represent potential danger for you and your financial future. Most of the red flags result from techniques that are used by advisors to win your trust, win your assets, and maximize their incomes. The ultimate danger occurs when the advisors use the techniques to create flattering but deceptive pictures of their credentials, services, and expenses. The result is that you select a weak professional and place your financial future in jeopardy.

Following are several of the most common red flags.

Verbal Presentations

A classic red flag is a presentation that is completely verbal—nothing is in writing. In extreme cases, the professional resists providing any support documentation that proves the claims of competence, integrity, and results, because the written information would conflict with what the individual has said.

Initials

Many advisors have accumulated an impressive array of initials after their names. In extreme cases, it is a bit like alphabet soup. The advisors use the initials as a testament to their knowledge. In other words, you should hire them because they have more initials than other professionals you are considering. If you are going to place importance on initials, you must research their validity and value to help you achieve your financial goals.

Registered Investment Advisors

You should be suspicious of professionals who are not Registered Investment Advisors (RIAs) or are not part of an RIA company. You always want RIA advisors handling your assets, because they have fiduciary status and are subject to increased disclosure requirements. They are also required to put your interests first. The financial services industry has continuously fought the RIA requirement for advisors because it makes them more accountable for the quality of their services.

Licensing

There is a high probability that an advisor who is only Series 6 and insurance licensed is a sales representative who makes a living marketing investment products. The Series 6 is a low-level license that only permits the sale of financial products. This is a major red flag because you do not want sales professionals influencing or controlling your financial future. They are paid to sell products and their principal motivation is earning the maximum amount of commissions from your assets. If this were not their motivation, they would be fee-based advisors.

Hedge Words

One of the most common techniques in the financial services industry is the use of hedge words to change the meaning of information. That is, some advisors might make strong statements to create a good impression and then use hedge words to make them more acceptable to compliance officers and regulators. There are several words that occur more often than others in sales literature, proposals, RFIs (Request For Information), and the presentations of financial advisors. Frequently used hedge words include *believe*, *possibly*, *may*, *should*, *could*, *try*, *attempt*, and *might*. For example, you hear or read the following phrase used to describe a track record: "We believe this information accurately portrays our record." What is wrong with this statement? Well, either the information is accurate or it is not. The hedged statement reduces the legitimacy of the record. A quality advisor will not use hedge words except as required by regulators.

The Redirected Response

There is also the redirected response technique that occurs when advisors choose not to answer your questions. Instead, they change the topic and attempt to redirect your attention to another, usually unrelated area. For example, you might ask about the performance of client accounts since the beginning of the year, and the advisor responds with a lengthy description of the market's performance. This professional never answers the question you asked about client accounts because the truth might be bad. An accurate response would cost the advisor your assets. How do you trust professionals with your financial future when they will not provide honest, direct responses to your questions?

Name Dropping

Another deceptive tactic that advisors use is to drop names of individuals or companies who have high visibility in your community. This may impress you, but there is a major red flag associated with this sales technique. First of all, the advisor may not even have a relationship with the person in question, or the advisor could be responsible for only a small portion of the named person's assets. You do not know for sure what the relationship is and you have no way of finding out—unless the relationship is documented and the person is named as a reference.

You should also listen to the language that the advisor uses, because the named person may have terminated the services years ago. For example, advisors may say that they have worked with big names in your community. However, "have worked" is the past tense, so you cannot be certain that there are current relationships. You should ask how long ago the advisor worked with these individuals and why the relationships were terminated.

You should be aware that most advisory agreements with investors have confidentiality clauses. An advisor who name drops is actually violating these client agreements. The practice lacks integrity and is a red flag.

Hot Performers

The number one technique for professionals with limited investment advisory skills is to sell products based on historical performance. High historical returns are, naturally, easier to sell than low returns. The high returns also appeal to those investors who mistakenly believe that strong track records are synonymous with high performance in the future.

It also requires a substantial amount of knowledge to explain why it may be smarter to invest in a product that is currently out of favor with the market. Advisors would have to understand why it is not performing as well as other products and be able to explain the reasons to you. As a result, it is always easier to sell performance, even though there may be significant evidence that future returns will not be the same as past returns.

Risk Versus Return

The higher the returns you expect, the more risk you will have to take to achieve them. However, this is not the way that some advisors present risk when they are selling products. A red flag goes up when the advisors suggest that they can produce high returns and low risk from the same investments. This is absolutely not possible—the markets are too efficient to let that happen.

Fixed Income Strategy

Most advisors know that it is hard to justify a fee when your assets are invested in the bond market. For example, it is hard to justify two percent fees for an asset class that returns six percent per year. The fee is one-third of the return, and it reduces your net return to four percent, that is, before you pay taxes on the six percent and your return is reduced to less than three percent. Distribute the income to cover living expenses and add inflation to the mix and you may have a negative rate of return. You may find that at some point the advisor is making more than you are on the investment—a major red flag.

The Concierge

Be wary of advisors who offer services that are outside the scope of what is considered normal for an investment professional. A recent version of this offering is the advent of *concierge* advisors. You give them your assets and they provide a broad range of unrelated services. High-quality advisors do not provide these non-investment services. They are focused on providing investment services that positively impact your financial future. Do not forget that the role of the advisor is to help you achieve your financial goals, not plan your next vacation.

Telephone Solicitation

Never under any circumstances invest your assets with an advisor who solicits your business over the telephone. Quality advisors do not market their services this way. Only new or substandard professionals use this process to generate sales and there is a high probability that the products are inferior or outright junk. You should always require advisors to complete the due diligence process which includes one or more in-person meetings.

Cheap Can Be Expensive

There are no free services, but there are less expensive ones. For example, you interview four advisors and three charge similar fees, while one is substantially less expensive. Will you receive the same quality of service from the less expensive professional?

Lower-cost services are increasingly prominent in the financial services industry due to competitive pressures. However, when this happens, all advisors lower their fees in response to the pressure. In the above example, only one out of four advisors charged lower prices, and that is the red flag. This advisor is likely less experienced than the others and is using the lower cost strategy to compete with superior advisors. This may be the only strategic advantage that this professional has, lacking the credentials to compete on a qualitative basis.

Cheap is the most expensive advice there is. You still pay for it, only it is in the form of underperformance rather than a fee or commission. You should be extremely vigilant when fees appear to be low on a relative basis.

The Deal

The North American Securities Administrators Association says to watch out for dishonest brokers who tell you about a "once-in-a-lifetime" opportunity, especially when the callers base the recommendation on "inside" or "confidential" information.

Some advisors may offer you deals designed to speed up your selection process—another classic red flag. In other words, the sooner you make a decision, the sooner they win your assets and receive their compensation for the sale. Here are a few examples of red flag deals:

- "The mutual fund or other product is about to close." The truth is that there are thousands of products to choose from. You should never rush.
- "If you make your decision today, I can get you the product for a lower fee." Financial product companies rarely raise fees. They generate additional revenue by increasing market values and winning new assets.
- "The market is at or near a bottom, so you should hurry to get in." Do not fall for this; no professional has access to a crystal ball which is that accurate.

Sometimes, the real urgency of the deal is to qualify your assets for a contest, to meet a quota, or simply to earn the income the sale will produce that month. Whatever their real reason might be, you should avoid deals that rush your decisions.

Sales Avoidance

Experienced but unscrupulous advisors with something to hide will not refuse to provide the information you are seeking. Instead, they will use their sales skills to convince you that the information you requested is unnecessary or unimportant. Regardless of the tactic, they have refused to provide responses to specific questions and should be excluded from further consideration. The nondisclosure of important information is a major red flag which should never be ignored.

The Insurance Solution

Advisors who recommend insurance products for all of your investment needs are suspect. These products rarely provide superior management for your assets. What they have in common is exceptionally high commission rates when compared to other investment products. In addition, there is a high probability that the professional is an insurance agent with a securities license who is employed or contracted by a company that is focused on the sale of insurance products.

Inexperience and Leveraged Relationships

Another red flag is the lack of advisor expertise. For example, do casualty insurance agents possess the knowledge to provide high quality investment advice? Very few have received sufficient training or possess credentials that establish them as experts. In most cases, investments are a way for companies and advisors to leverage their relationships with you by marketing additional products that produce incremental revenue streams.

The "Blame-the-Market" Technique

Your advisor has had four consecutive quarters of bad performance. In each quarterly meeting, the advisor blames the market for the underperformance. In other words, it is somehow the market's fault that you are lagging—you were in domestic stocks when you should have been invested in international stocks, for example. This is a red flag because you are paying advisors to recommend strategies and managers who beat the benchmarks. You are paying the advisor and managers significant fees to deliver superior results. If you are not getting results, you must take action to improve the situation.

Lack of Choice

A major red flag is raised when advisors provide proposals that limit your investment choices to proprietary products or a specific group of products. The limitation is frequently in the best interest of the advisors or their companies—not yours. The way that you identify choice limitations is to review the proposed strategies submitted by multiple advisors during the due diligence process. Proposal One limits your choice to proprietary products or a particular mutual fund family. Proposal Two uses the best managers from a number of families. The first proposal raises a red flag and you must question the limitations to determine if you are satisfied with the professional's response.

There are several strategies by which advisors limit your choices:

- Several mutual funds are recommended for investment, but they are all from one family.

- Multiple insurance products are recommended, but they are all from one insurance company.
- Advisors recommend particular money managers that are owned by their companies.

The Fifty Percent Rule

Some financial institutions have developed a more creative and less detectable way to restrict your choices to certain products. Your advisor can recommend any money managers they prefer for one-half of your assets, as long as the other half goes to "preferred" products that are usually selected by the company.

This strategy has the *appearance* of unrestricted choice. Fifty percent of your assets are still restricted to particular products, however, whether they are the best investments or not. Companies that do this have concluded that it is better to win half the time with higher-margin products than to have 100 percent of sales go to lower-margin third party products. This is a serious conflict when the restriction produces lower net returns for your assets. Regardless of the reasons you are given, any form of limitation is bad. You want unlimited choice so you can pick the best managers for your assets.

The Good Guys

It is important to point out that thousands of advisors do not give into conflicts of interest. Instead, they are focused on providing services that have one purpose: to help you achieve your financial goals. These advisors are paid fees that are based on the market value of your assets. If the value goes down, they take a pay cut. If they do not meet expectations over time, you terminate their services and their income stops. Their principal strategies for building substantial personal incomes are high client retention rates and market appreciation. A high retention rate means that your needs are being met. One way to show appreciation for a job well done is to tell your family, friends, and associates. People you know are always looking for a quality advisor.

Quality advisors are also more than happy to provide written disclosures of important information you need to make your selection decisions. They have nothing to hide, so the information is easy for you to obtain. Advisors who have something to hide will resist the disclosure process.

SUMMARY

- The financial services industry is one of the most conflicted industries in America because a sales culture permeates it. Instead, the culture should be one of value-added advice.

- All advisors have potential conflicts of interest. Do they do what is best for you? Or what is best for themselves and their companies?

- Conflicts of interest are a way of doing business for most financial advisors. They do not think twice about putting their interests ahead of yours. The practices are legal and acceptable because virtually all of their competitors have the same conflicts.

- Companies and regulators will not protect your financial interests— they have their own conflicts. You must learn to protect your own interests.

- The advisors' personal integrity is what protects you from these conflicts. However, their trustworthiness can be difficult to measure in advance.

- The way you protect your interests is to be aware of the conflicts described in this chapter, factor it into your selection process, and monitor the quality of the professional's advice.

- Anytime you experience a conflict, you should immediately terminate the relationship. There may be other conflicts that you do not know about.

5

CRITERIA

I have described why selecting a competent, trustworthy advisor is a critical part of your strategy to accumulate sufficient assets for retirement. In addition, I have detailed the substantial risk to which you are exposed in the advisor selection process, because I believe three-fourths of all advisors provide services of questionable quality and expense. Choosing an advisor should be an analytical process focused on evaluating competency and integrity. To maximize your probability of success, the process must be based on data that you control—not what is contained in advisor presentations. When professionals control data, you cannot count on receiving the critical information you need to make a positive selection decision. To initiate the process, you must become familiar with the most important criteria, so you know what you are looking for. Then you can obtain the information from several advisors and compare their responses.

Educational Background

Like all professionals, advisors are in the knowledge business. They charge substantial fees and commissions for applying their knowledge to your financial situation. In fact, if they did not possess specialized investment expertise, there would be no reason to hire them. If you are like most investors, you assume that all licensed advisors have a minimum amount of education to be employed in the financial services industry—just like doctors, lawyers, CPAs, and other professionals. This very dangerous assumption can seriously endanger your financial future.

The financial services industry has a very different standard when compared to other industries. Its standard is based on a sales culture that serves the industry's interests and not yours. This self-serving culture does not include minimum educational requirements.

The Importance of Education

Education is one of two primary processes for acquiring knowledge; the other is experience. As a result, you have to assume that education increases the knowledge levels of advisors so they can provide higher quality services for your assets. Since it is very difficult to measure knowledge, it is critical that you evaluate their education. You must review the various types of educational programs that have been completed by the advisor. At the very least, this will provide you with some confidence that the prospective advisor has gone through a formal learning process as part of his or her background.

Industry Requirements

The industry does not require financial advisors to have any formal education—not even a high school diploma. Any requirements that exist are based on company standards, not industry standards. Some firms require college degrees while others do not. Virtually all firms will make exceptions for individuals who lack formal education if they possess strong sales and relationship skills. This means that a high percentage of advisors may not be as educated as you thought they were. Therefore, you have to ask very specific questions in order to ascertain the advisor's educational background.

College Education

A college education should be the first criterion on your list when evaluating advisors. A solid scholastic background with an appropriate major is an important part of an advisor's knowledge base. All advisors should have a four-year college degree for the same reason that doctors should have a degree. Medicine and financial services are both knowledge-based professions that impact the quality of your life—physical health and financial health. A college degree is an indicator of an advisor's attitude towards learning. The degree is an investment by the advisor who wishes to increase his or her knowledge base and value to you. It should be noted, however, that there are some excellent advisors who provide very high quality services but who never completed college. These advisors, who are exceptions to the rule, must offset their lack of formal education with experience, certifications, and other industry-specific learning programs.

Advanced degrees are even more telling than undergraduate degrees because they are evidence of an even higher commitment to knowledge. They also usually indicate that the advisor has the work ethic to complete demanding scholastic programs. In addition, many advanced degrees include substantial coursework in investment-related topics.

The most appropriate majors for the financial services industry are finance (investment, not accounting), economics, and business. Alternative degrees are not all bad, but they do not contribute to an advisor's financial knowledge base as much as these three.

Diploma Mills

Advisors realize that investors prefer professionals with college educations, especially those with advanced degrees. Some less scrupulous professionals are not above buying the degrees from so-called diploma mills to impress you. The Internet has spawned thousands of these "institutions"—they offer post secondary degrees, diplomas, or certificates but lack accreditation. Diploma mills confer immediate degrees for little or no work—just money. I recommend checking out unfamiliar schools with recognized accreditation organizations, for example, *www.acics.org*, *www.aacsb.edu*, *www.ed.gov*, and *www.chea.org*. You can also visit the school's website to determine if it offers degrees for experience, self-study, or a fee. Automatically exclude advisors with diploma-mill degrees from your selection process. If you cannot trust their educations, how can you trust their advice?

Continuing Education

Virtually all financial industry licensing, certifications, and associations have continuing education programs that mandate a certain number of hours each year. The result is that the longer advisors are in the industry, the more knowledgeable they should be.

Because these continuing education programs are required for the maintenance of active licenses, designations, and association memberships, advisors should have a record of them that can be provided to you. You should ask what the required number of education hours is each year and ask for descriptions of the courses that they have taken over the past three years. The course selection will also provide some insight into the specializations and interests of the advisors.

Apprenticeships

The financial services industry does not require any type of apprenticeships to help new advisors acquire knowledge from experienced professionals. The companies want them selling products to investors as soon as possible to maximize revenues and profits. This reality increases the risk of bad advice when you select a newly licensed professional to be your advisor.

You will occasionally meet junior advisors who work with or for senior advisors. Although this relationship is strictly voluntary, it should be a requirement to enter the industry. Unfortunately, companies place more emphasis on selling than knowledge. Advisors who completed apprenticeships may provide higher quality services sooner in their careers than those advisors who did not. At a minimum, they have had an opportunity to accelerate their learning by working with more experienced professionals.

Investment Experience

There is only one reason why you should hire an investment professional and pay that individual substantial fees to help you achieve your goals: the advisor can produce higher net returns than you can achieve on your own. Competence, based on substantial knowledge, makes that happen. We already know that investing is extraordinarily complex because it is more of an art than a science. It takes years of experience to develop the competence that enables a professional to become a qualified artist in the investment world.

Years of Experience

You should require your advisor to have a documented minimum of five years of experience that includes investment training, certification programs, and experience working with asset amounts similar to yours. Generally speaking, the more experience your advisor has, the better. After ten years, however, the quantity of experience is less important than the quality of experience. The financial services industry is frequently referred to as a "pay for gray" industry because older advisors with higher experience levels are usually more qualified than younger advisors with less experience.

Age

The assumption that age automatically equals experience can endanger your financial future. For example, many advisors may have had careers in other industries before entering financial services. A 40-year-old advisor may have only a few weeks of financial services experience, while a 30-year-old advisor may have 12 years of experience—the minimum age is 18. Do not assume a certain amount of experience based solely on the advisor's age. It pays to ask very specific questions about how many years your potential advisor has spent in the financial industry.

Quality Versus Quantity

Years measure time but tell you nothing about the quality of an advisor's experience. You have to use other data to determine this, such as number of clients, longevity of clients, number of client complaints, and assets under management. All of these provide some insight into the successful application of an advisor's experience.

The quality of advice is also heavily influenced by an advisor's experience in a variety of market and economic conditions. For example, does the advisor have experience in rising, falling, and flat markets? Has the advisor experienced high growth, flat, and recession years?

Company Names

The company name on the door has nothing to do with the experience levels of its advisors. However, it is reasonable to expect that new advisors with brand name companies will have more training opportunities than new independent advisors who are self-employed. Also, keep in mind that many independent advisors used to be employees of brand name firms. You should never forget that you are hiring the advisor, not the firm. Advisors have a tremendous amount of latitude when they make investment recommendations for your assets. This latitude creates the need for knowledge and integrity on the advisor's part. However, if the advisor works for an unethical firm, odds are that the advisor is also unethical. Adequate knowledge may not exist, but it does not matter. You and your assets are in serious trouble.

Job Titles

Be careful when using titles to assess seniority and experience. At some companies, titles may be the reward for advisors with strong sales results. At other companies, though, titles can be a reflection of an advisor's true ability to offer higher quality financial solutions based on client needs. Independent advisors frequently use very lofty titles such as president, managing director, or chief investment officer. However, since they are frequently the only professionals in their companies, they can assume any title they want. Their selection may be designed to impress you and may not be an indication of their actual levels of experience or responsibilities.

Related Experience

Very few professions provide experience that is useful in the financial services industry. Two exceptions are tax and legal backgrounds. A percentage of your assets are likely to be subject to taxation, so you would benefit from the experience of an advisor who is a former CPA. Assets in trusts would also benefit from the knowledge of a former estate attorney.

Securities Licenses

On the one hand, financial services is one of the most regulated industries in the country. On the other hand, regulators do very little to protect investors from bad advisors—especially when "bad" is a result of incompetence and lapses of integrity. Having said that, the regulatory agencies provide information which you can use to evaluate advisor integrity. One of their principal responsibilities is the issuance of licenses that companies and advisors must keep in good standing to continue providing financial services to you. They also maintain websites that provide the compliance histories of advisors. It is important for you to know the implications of the various types of securities and advisory licenses and their impact on the service offerings of financial advisors.

Licenses Make a Difference

The licenses held by advisors will tell you the types of services that they are able to provide and the types of compensation that they can receive for those services. For example, advisors cannot offer fee-based advice, nor can they receive fee-based compensation, if they are not properly licensed. The only exception is solicitors, who receive fees that result from their referrals to financial professionals.

The Regulatory Agencies

There are several types of agencies that issue licenses for the sale of financial products and services:

- The National Association of Securities Dealers (NASD) and National Association of Securities Administrators Association (NASAA) regulate all securities licenses including Series 6, 7, 24, 63, and 65. The NASD is a self-regulatory organization comprised of member firms. The NASAA is comprised of state regulators.
- The Securities & Exchange Commission (SEC) issues the national Registered Investment Advisor (RIA) registrations to individuals or companies who have more than $25 million under their control.
- Various state agencies issue RIA registrations to individuals or companies who have less than $25 million of assets; they also issue all insurance licenses.

Securities Licenses

The NASD issues the licenses that advisors need to sell financial products. The licenses are as follows:

- Series 7: A general-purpose securities license that enables professionals to be compensated for trading securities and selling financial products for commissions. The Series 7 replaces the need for the Series 6, 22, 52, 42, 62, and 72 licenses.
- Series 63: A uniform securities agent state law license that enables advisors to market services and products in their home state and other states where they are properly licensed.
- Series 65: A license for fee-based advisors.
- Series 66: A uniform state license that combines the Series 63 and Series 65.
- Series 6: A securities license that limits advisors to the sale of mutual funds and variable insurance products such as annuities and universal life. Sales of insurance products also require insurance licenses.
- Series 24: The general securities principal's license for supervising licensed professionals.
- Series 3: Permits the sale of commodities.
- Series 4: Permits the supervision of option licensed professionals.
- Series 22: Permits the sale of direct participation programs.
- Series 42: Permits the sale of options contracts.
- Series 52: Permits the sale of municipal securities.
- Series 53: Permits the supervision of municipal licensed professionals.
- Series 62: Permits the sale of corporate securities.
- Series 72: Permits the sale of government securities.

In addition to securities licenses, a high percentage of advisors hold insurance licenses that are issued by state commissioners. The various insurance licenses are as follows:

- Fixed annuity: An insurance license that enables advisors to market fixed annuity products. This license also covers other fixed insurance products.
- Variable annuity: An insurance license that enables advisors to market variable annuity products, a process that also requires a Series 6 or 7 license.
- Life insurance: An insurance license that enables professionals to market life insurance products and fixed annuities.

- Variable life insurance: An insurance license that enables advisors to market variable life insurance products, a process that also requires a Series 6 or 7 license.

You always want to be cautious when entering into a new relationship, but I recommend being particularly cautious when advisors are not licensed to receive fees for their services. When advisors are limited to earning commissions, there is a high likelihood that the advisor is a sales professional. You do not want a sales professional influencing investment decisions which will determine your financial future. When you interview a prospective advisor, you should determine what licenses the advisor has, how long the advisor has held them, and what the record of compliance with applicable regulations has been.

Registered Investment Advisors

The ideal type of advisor will be one who is a Registered Investment Advisor (RIA) or works for a company that is an RIA firm. This type of advisor can act in a fiduciary capacity, has additional disclosure requirements, and can provide discretionary or nondiscretionary services for your assets.

If you are considering an RIA—either an individual or company—then you will want to see their ADV Part II and the schedule of fees they charge for their services. A published ADV is required for all RIAs by either the SEC or the states. Vital information about the individual and the firm is contained in these documents, and it is imperative that you review the contents before making your selection.

Compliance

The only way to avoid hiring unethical advisors is to check their compliance records with the various regulatory agencies. You will need their full names or Central Registry Depository (CRD) number to check for securities violations and investor complaints. You will also need their insurance license numbers to complete your compliance checks.

The NASD (*www.nasdr.com*), NASAA (*www.nasaa.org*), IARD (*www.iard.com*), and SEC (*www.sec.gov*) post the compliance histories of financial advisors on the Internet. You can review the advisors' complete compliance histories and receive a report for no charge and draw your own conclusions about their trustworthiness. All regulatory agencies strongly recommend that you check compliance histories before investing assets.

Designations

One way that advisors display knowledge is by listing an impressive array of initials after their names. But do these designations provide any real benefits to you? Will they have a positive impact on the performance of your assets? Will they help you achieve your financial goals? Or, is their real purpose to impress you enough to win your assets? The answer to all of these questions is "maybe."

The most important issue is the initial and continuing learning experience the professional went through to earn and retain the designations. Your challenge is to differentiate between high- and low-quality certification programs that offer designations and determine their importance in your selection process.

Designation Criteria

There are certain criteria you should look for when assessing the value of designations:

- The background of the issuing board, agency or association
- The longevity of the issuer
- The business purpose of the issuer
- The knowledge associated with the designation
- The experience requirement for earning the designation
- The amount of coursework required to earn the designation
- The amount of time it takes to earn the designation
- The determination of whether the examination was proctored or self-administered
- The failure rate for examinations
- The continuing education requirements
- The ethical requirements for holding the designation

Types of Certifications

If your hiring decisions will be influenced by designations, then I would recommend investigating them. Information about certification programs is available on the Internet. Ask the professional whom you are interviewing for the web address and evaluate the requirements for earning the designation. The professional should receive your respect and possibly your assets if the designation required a serious amount of work and improved the advisor's ability to help you achieve your goals.

Examples of investment and insurance certifications include the following:

- Chartered Financial Analyst (CFA)—Securities analysis
- Chartered Investment Management Analyst (CIMA)—Money manager analysis
- Certified Financial Planner (CFP®)—Comprehensive financial plans
- Certified Fund Specialist (CFS)—Mutual Funds
- Certified Investment Management Consultant (CIMC)—Analysis of mutual funds and separate account money managers
- Certified Investment Strategist (CIS)—Advanced investment, tax, and legal strategies
- Certified Public Accountant (CPA)—Tax preparation and audit services
- Chartered Life Underwriter (CLU)—Life insurance
- Chartered Financial Consultant (ChFC)—Financial planning designation for insurance agents
- Chartered Retirement Plans Specialist (CRPS®)—Pension plans
- Chartered Retirement Planning Specialist (CRPC®)—Retirement plans
- Certified Trust & Financial Advisor (CTFA)—Estate planning and trust expertise
- Personal Financial Specialist (PFS)—Planning designation for CPAs
- Registered Financial Consultant (RFC)—Investment strategy

Holding Periods

The value of designations should be measured in years—especially if they have continuing education requirements. An advisor who has been a CIMA for five years has more relative value than someone who just received the designation.

Combinations

A significant number of professional hold more than one designation that cover various fields of specialized study. For example, one ideal planning combination is a CPA/PFS. There are only 2,500 professionals with this combination and you should seek them out for their planning and tax expertise. According to *Worth* magazine's 2002 List of Top Financial Advisors, nearly 25 percent are CPAs and almost 20 percent also hold the PFS designation. This is high praise for such a small group of professionals.

Association Memberships

Membership in associations should also be an important criterion for your advisor selection process. Advisor memberships display commitment to the profession, to continuing education, and to developing relationships inside the industry.

Integrity and Education

Being a member of reputable industry associations that promote integrity and significant amounts of continuing education is an indicator of an advisor's commitment to the profession. Many of these associations have developed bylaws that describe their membership requirements for integrity. In addition, they make continuing education a requirement for membership. In general, the odds of hiring an ethical, knowledgeable advisor are increased if the professional is a member in good standing with one or more reputable associations.

Officer Roles

You should give additional credit to advisors who hold officer positions in associations and/or can show active involvement on committees. For example, Jim Smith is the president of his local chapter of the American Association of Financial Advisors. This is a higher commitment than membership alone and usually represents recognition by peers. It also implies good standing with the association bylaws and membership guidelines.

Associations

Some of the most prominent advisor associations are:

- Investment Management Consultants Association—*www.imca.org*
- National Association of Investment Professionals—*www.naip.com*
- Association of Investment Management & Research—*www. aimr.com*
- National Association of Personal Financial Advisors—*www. napfa.org*
- Financial Planning Association—*www.fpanet.org*
- Certified Financial Planner Board of Standards—*www.cfp-board.org*
- International Association of Registered Financial Consultants—*www.iarfc.org*

Preferred Method of Compensation

One of the most controversial topics in the financial services industry is the appropriate way to pay for financial advice. At the core of the controversy are advisors who still cling to outdated ways of doing business: giving away knowledge and charging commissions for the sale of financial products and transactions. Advisors who are more service-oriented are the opposite—they are compensated for their knowledge with a fee and do not charge commissions.

Compensation is a recurring topic in this book because it is a critical component of the selection process. It can affect the type of services you receive as well as the quality of those services. It may also be a major source of conflicts of interest.

Source of Payment

Broker/dealers pay commissions for securities transactions. Financial product companies pay commissions for the sale of their mutual funds, annuities, and life insurance products. Only you can pay fees, which are deducted from your accounts. Because there is a choice, a critical question is whether you want third parties compensating the professionals who provide investment recommendations that will determine your financial future. In effect, whether or not you achieve your goals depends on the revenue needs of third parties—a major conflict of interest if there ever was one.

Commissions

There is a good reason why financial service companies refer to representatives as their "sales force" or "distribution system." Their historical role has been to sell products. This is particularly true when the advisors are compensated with commissions, a payment system with one purpose: to provide quick rewards for the sale of financial products. The typical commission is four to five percent, but can be much higher.

The product companies use several strategies for paying commissions, often referred to as sales loads. In some cases, the payment methods are designed to hide commissions or at least make them less obvious to inexperienced investors. Products are more marketable when commission amounts are not a primary topic of discussion. Following are examples of commission types:

- *Front-end loads (A Shares).* The four- to five-percent commission payment is deducted from your assets when you invest in the products.
- *Back-end loads (B Shares).* Commissions are paid at the time of the sale by the product companies. This type of load is not deducted from your assets as is a front-end load; however, the companies recover their commission payments by increasing the fees they deduct from your accounts. They protect their prepayment of the commissions to the advisor by assessing penalties for early termination, thereby reducing the liquidity of your assets.
- *Level loads (C Shares).* Rather than one large load payment (four to five percent), the payment is spread out over a period of years and does not change. This type of load is more favorable to you than front-end loads, because more of your assets are invested and the advisor has an incentive to service your portfolio.

- *Trailers*. Similar to level loads, trailers are a continuous commission that is paid for the life of relationship. This type of load is also more favorable to you compared to the alternatives.
- *Finder's fees*. Some product companies use a portion of their revenue to pay finder's fees to advisors. These fees are usually associated with the movement of larger sums of assets.
- *12B-1 Fees*. Mutual funds can assess a 12B-1 fee, which is a way for them to recoup some of their marketing costs at your expense. Certain funds pay that fee to financial service companies and their representatives.

Fees

The other popular method for compensating financial professionals for their advice is a fee. The fee is most frequently expressed as a percentage of the market value of your assets. For example, a one percent fee on $500,000 is $5,000 per year. When your assets appreciate to $1 million dollars, the fee increases to $10,000. As your assets continue to grow, fees decline as a percentage of assets due to the breakpoints of declining fee schedules. Fees may also be expressed in basis points rather than percentages. For example, one percent is one hundred basis points (bps). A basis point is 1/100 of one percent.

Financial planners may also charge fees for their services. For them, the fee is usually fixed—for example, $2,500. Some planners may charge hourly fees, especially for more complex plans, when it is difficult to estimate the amount of time necessary to complete the plan.

Sliding Schedules of Fees

All providers of fee-based financial services offer discounts to investors with larger asset amounts. They do this by using a sliding schedule of fees. For example, an advisor might charge a one percent fee for $250,000 of invested assets and a .5 percent fee for $1 million. The advisor is still rewarded for working with the larger asset amount because the fee doubled from $2,500 to $5,000—the assets increased by four times and the fee increased by two times. This is the impact of a sliding schedule of fees.

Investor Preferences

Investor preferences for paying advisors were measured in a joint survey conducted by the VIP Forum and Spectrem Group in 2002. The respondents were given four choices:

1. Pay a commission for each product purchased or transaction conducted
2. Pay a flat fee for each transaction or product purchased
3. Pay an all-encompassing flat fee for all transactions or purchases
4. Pay an asset-based, all encompassing fee based on the amount of assets

Following are the results of their survey:

- 55 percent found the "all-encompassing flat fee" as the most attractive structure
- 47 percent found "flat fee" as attractive
- 35 percent found "asset based all-encompassing fee" attractive
- 27 percent found "commission" attractive

Commissions came in a distant fourth to the fee alternatives. Why, then, do so many investors pay commissions? It is simple: they were never given the choices described in the survey by their advisors.

Advisor Motivation

Sales-oriented advisors prefer commissions as the method of payment for five principal reasons. First, they can be paid upfront at the time of the sale. Second, commissions are much larger than their portion of a fee, usually by a ratio of 4:1 or higher. Third, since advisors have been paid upfront for their services, they have no downside if you terminate them. Fourth, when product companies pay the commissions, you may think the advisor's services are free. Fifth, the advisor does not have to do any additional work to earn the commissions.

Your alternative is fee advisors who require recurring income because they provide continuous services. They are always involved after the sale, because their future income is based on meeting your expectations; otherwise, you will terminate their services and their revenue stops.

Full Disclosure

One of the most critical questions that you must ask during the selection process concerns the method and amount of compensation for the financial professionals' services. You want every dollar that they earn from their relationship with you to be fully disclosed in advance and in writing. It will be much easier for you to trust advisors with your financial future when you make clear the services you will receive and the advisors' compensation for providing those services. Once you know how much advisors are being paid for their advice, you can make an informed decision about which advisors provide the best value for the lowest cost.

Selling Versus Advising

Another major difference between fees and commissions is the frequency of payment. Most commissions are a one-time occurrence and are paid upfront at the time of the sale. For commission representatives to earn continuous income, they must generate new sales every month. This means that they are more focused on selling than servicing what they have already sold.

Fee-based advisors, however, do not have to create product sales and buy/sell transactions to be paid. They are paid a continuous fee, based on your asset amount, for their ongoing services, and the fees are not dependent on the sale of additional products. Instead of selling, they can focus on helping you achieve your financial goals. This becomes a win-win situation for you and the advisor.

Hidden Compensation

Some compensation payments to advisors are easy to identify, while others are hidden from your view. For example, fees are easy to see because they are deducted from your account each quarter. Front-end loads are easy to see, because they are deducted from your initial asset amounts. Back-end loads are more difficult to identify because they are taken from the fees that you pay for the management and administration of the products.

Certain mutual fund companies also pay finder's fees that are totally separate from their product fees. These revenue-sharing strategies are designed to hide the true compensation of the professionals and the companies they work for. This way, you cannot compare value to expense, and advisors can be paid incentives to market particular products.

There are also "soft dollar" arrangements, whereby a product company agrees to trade securities through an account that benefits an advisor or company. These hidden commissions compensate advisors for placing your assets in particular products. Lower-quality product providers employ these tactics to motivate less scrupulous advisors to market their products because they have to.

Because they cannot see the compensation, too many inexperienced investors believe the services are free. This provides a competitive advantage to advisors whose principal goal is to maximize the amount of money they earn from your assets and still "appear" to provide inexpensive services.

Asset Amounts

Another important selection criterion involves the dollar amount of assets you place with an advisor and how that amount compares to the average asset size of the advisor's other clients. You want this information because good advisors allocate their time based on the amount of revenue that they can generate per client. You want to know the level of service you can expect given the assets you own. In addition, if you have a larger asset amount, you want to be sure that the advisor is experienced servicing asset amounts of your size. Service expectations and the service actually delivered may differ unless you obtain this information during your fact-finding.

Average Assets

You want to ensure that the amount of assets you place with the advisor is large enough to make you an important client. If you invest $400,000 with an advisor whose average client invests $2 million, you may experience a reduced service level because you represent less revenue to the advisor. The opposite is also true. You may experience a very high level of service when you invest $5 million with an advisor whose average client invests $2 million.

Another way to measure your importance to advisors is to ask for the range of asset amounts that they service by client. For example, if their answer is $500,000 to $5,000,000 and you have $400,000 to invest, some advisors may not be willing to work with you. Even if your asset amount is within their average range but at the low end ($500,000, for example), you may have a problem getting some advisors to work with you. It pays to ask how your asset amount compares to their other clients.

Minimum Account Size

Minimum account sizes for fee-based services vary by company and advisor—all advisors at a particular company do not have the same minimums. The most common minimums are $100,000, $250,000, $500,000, and $1 million. Some are higher, but minimums of $1 million dollars or greater usually apply to institutional accounts, such as pension plans, and very high net worth individuals.

There are also advisors who have no minimum requirements. They are generally newer to the industry and/or have had limited success attracting assets from investors. As a result, they will take virtually any client who will hire them. This creates additional risk for investors with smaller asset amounts. They are the target market for advisors who are new, sales-oriented, and who possess a relatively low level of skill.

Advisor Service Levels

It stands to reason that investors with millions of dollars receive a higher level of service than investors with a few hundred thousand dollars. The important question that advisors must answer for you is how much service you will receive based on the amount of assets you place under their advisement. You want to know the parameters of the relationship upfront:

- Number of meetings per year
- Method of contact: face-to-face, telephone, Internet
- Accessibility between meetings
- Frequency of reports
- Timeliness of communications when there are problems

Before Versus After

You should always obtain information about an advisor's asset base before disclosing your amount of assets. This prevents them from modifying their answers. For example, you volunteer that you have $300,000 of assets. You then ask the advisor's minimum and the response is "$250,000." Had you asked for the minimum without divulging what you have to invest, the answer might have been $500,000. Advisors who are seeking assets will frequently lower their stated minimum to win the sale. The service level after the sale, however, may be questionable.

Service After the Sale

Successful commission-based advisors may have hundreds or even thousands of clients, so how can they possibly provide a comparable level of service for all of their clients? The answer is that they cannot. Commission advisors provide little or no service after the sale. The larger client bases facilitate the marketing of a high volume of financial products because the clients are prospects for additional sales.

On the other hand, successful fee-based advisors work with fewer clients who, on average, own larger asset amounts. Unlike their commission-based counterparts, they do not require extremely large client bases to generate new sales from month to month. They receive continuous compensation for providing ongoing services, so they can afford to spend more time with a smaller number of clients.

Grading Client Relationships

Just about every successful advisor grades clients on an A-B-C scale. The A clients are those who generate the most current revenue or have the potential to generate the most future revenue. The B clients produce smaller amounts of current revenue or smaller amounts of future revenue. In some cases, B clients have the potential to become A clients. C clients have the smallest amounts of assets and little or no opportunity for additional assets. As advisors become more successful, they frequently turn their C clients over to junior advisors in their offices. It is imperative that you know whether you are an A, B, or C client in the eyes of each advisor you are considering.

Junior Advisors

The most successful advisors frequently have junior associates who are responsible for servicing investors with smaller amounts of assets— the Cs. Senior advisors leverage their time while maximizing the amount of assets and number of investors that they can work with using this strategy. Junior advisors can also participate in apprenticeship programs. These programs provide excellent learning opportunities for newer advisors who want to gain experience working with larger, more complex asset amounts sooner than they could on their own.

A relationship with a junior advisor is not necessarily bad, as long as your portfolio reflects the knowledge and judgment of the senior advisor. You just might receive a higher level of service for your assets even though you do not see the senior advisor as often.

Performance Reviews

You and your advisor should allocate the time to meet quarterly to review the markets, current strategy, and recent manager performance. By meeting four times per year, you can stay up to date on your results without spending an excessive amount of time analyzing the decisions of your managers. (After all, this is the advisor's job.)

At each quarterly meeting, you should review the results of the professional's advice. The review should cover all areas of advice: asset allocation, manager selection, transactions, timeliness of services, expenses, and recommendations for any changes that should be made to your portfolio.

Rebalancing

Rebalancing your portfolio is a main risk management technique. Let us assume you own the two primary asset classes: stocks and bonds. Based on your return objectives and tolerance for risk, your advisor recommends an original asset allocation of sixty percent stocks and forty percent bonds. One year later, because stocks outperformed bonds, the equity (stock) allocation is eighty percent and fixed income (bonds) is twenty percent. Your risk is increased because stocks are more volatile than bonds.

Your solution is to rebalance the portfolio to the original sixty-forty allocation. This strategy forces you to take gains from higher-performing investments. Keep in mind that the process is not as simple or painless as it may sound when your accounts are taxable. Rebalancing may produce taxable events you would prefer to defer—such as short-term capital gains. In addition, you will be selling higher- performing investments from the portfolio and buying lower-performing investments. However, your objective here is risk management and not performance. Rebalancing is an important strategy that requires careful thought and execution by skilled, knowledgeable professionals. Be sure that the advisor you select is willing to provide rebalancing services.

Accessibility

Another selection criterion should be the accessibility of the advisor or a member of the advisor's staff when you have questions or require distributions from your accounts. Advisors should be able to respond to your calls or emails in a timely fashion. You should expect a response within the same business day if your request is received before noon and a response the next morning for requests that are received after noon.

Monitoring

A very important service requirement is the advisor's ability to actively monitor your investments. This important function includes, but is not limited to, performance problems, style drift, transaction volume, cash levels, and risk exposure. Higher-level monitoring should include the provisions contained in the written investment policy that documents your expectations. For example, if your policy restricts investments in tobacco stocks, the advisor should monitor the purchases of the managers to make sure no tobacco stocks were bought for any of your accounts.

Bear Market Communications

Your advisor should be even more accessible during times of unsettled market conditions, such as short-term corrections or long-term down markets. You will likely have additional concerns fueled by fears that arise when your assets decline in value. An important role for your advisor is to provide a "steady hand" to help keep you from making emotional decisions that will undermine future results. Too many investors panic in the face of adversity and fail to recognize the opportunities that are produced by market volatility.

Support Services

Successful advisors use the services of various types of professional staff to leverage their time, support their sales efforts, and help them efficiently service their clientele. It is important for you to know the size of the staff supporting the advisors, the staff's credentials if they provide any type of advice, and their exact role in relation to your assets.

There is also the question of identifying the right person to call when you have particular types of problems. Advisors will delegate those duties to support staff so they can focus on providing services commensurate with their level of expertise.

Support Staff

Very few successful advisors can provide quality services for large numbers of clients by themselves. They use the services of support personnel to make the most of their time. The staff is mainly administrative, supporting sales and service activities. Some staff may be employees of the advisor. Other staff may be employees of the company that employs or licenses the advisor. It is important to distinguish between the two. If they are employees of the company, they may have additional duties that do not involve your advisor.

When an advisor refers to staff, it is important to obtain the following information:

- Are they dedicated to supporting the activities of the advisor?
- Are they located in the same office as the advisor or in the home office?
  - If they are local, you should meet them when conducting your due diligence visit to the advisors' offices.
- What is the exact role of each member of the staff?
- Who prepares proposed strategies for your assets: the staff or the advisor?

- Are any of the staff licensed professionals?
- What is the background of those who have responsibilities that may influence the performance, risk, or expense related to your assets?

Companies and Support

Your due diligence process should include companies that employ or license advisors for several reasons:

- The companies stand behind the advice of the advisors.
- The companies may own the liability insurance policies.
- The companies may be reputable or disreputable.
- The companies may be financially stable or unstable.
- The companies may influence the advice provided by your advisors.
- The companies may produce products that are integrated into advisor proposals.

You will usually rely on numbers to evaluate a company, looking at years in business, amount of assets under their control, number of employees, average assets per client, net capital, and other related information. The focus of the company's business strategy, its technological capabilities, and its philosophy in regard to financial products can also make a significant difference in the services that your advisor provides.

Total Expenses

An advisor's compensation is only one of several fees that is charged by the service providers. This is particularly important when advisors recommend services that produce layers of expenses for your assets. As you might imagine, there is a substantial expense range based on the quantity, quality, type, and name of the various service providers. Some advisors, custodians, and managers are more expensive than others.

Wrap Fees

A wrap fee is nothing more than a number of fees from various service providers that are "wrapped" into one fee. There are at least four primary services included in wrap advisory fees:

1. Money management
2. Custody and clearing services
3. Advisory services
4. Back office services

All of these service providers have to be paid and, in all cases, their fees are assessed as a percentage of the market value of your assets and are billed to your accounts.

Pay for Quality

Superior professionals should be able to charge higher fees than inferior ones. Although there are no guarantees, it stands to reason that "real" quality increases the probability that you will achieve your financial goals. Quality advisors have the knowledge to develop sophisticated strategies that will produce superior returns.

You should pay advisors according to their education, experience, and demonstrated expertise. To do that, you have to obtain their credentials to see if the compensation is warranted. Suffice it to say, there is a tremendous range in advisor quality. You would not want the majority of advisors handling your assets, even if they were really free.

References

References are the advisors' current clients or other professionals, such as CPAs or attorneys, who have had experience working with them. From your point of view, references provide a third party endorsement of the advisor's services. Advisors use references to allay any fears that you may have about the quality of their services.

References are the least important criterion for selecting advisors. If you are going to give references value, however, then you should be aware of one thing: most professionals develop relationships with individuals who will only make favorable comments about them.

Requested References

You must request references that fit particular criteria to increase the chances of receiving quality names. Good questions to ask include:

- If the advisor has been in business for ten years, what are the names of five references that have utilized his or her services for at least eight years?
- What are the names of the advisor's five largest clients as measured in assets?
- What are the names of clients who have objectives, risk tolerances, and asset amounts similar to your own?
- What are the names of clients who have terminated the advisors' services?

Resistance Levels

Another criterion that will help you determine the quality of advisors is their willingness to provide the names and phone numbers of current clients. If advisors are reluctant or unwilling to provide references, you should consider that a red flag. Newer advisors are the ones most likely not to have references.

Creative Questions

You can increase the value of references if you ask them very specific questions about their experiences with advisors. For example, how long has the professional been advising them? Have they ever had a really bad performance year? If yes, when and by how much? Who recommended the advisor to them? Did the advisor change firms during the relationship? What was his or her best recommendation? What was the worst recommendation?

Creative questions may give you better insight into the relationship between advisors and their references. The more creative the questions are, the better; the reference will most likely not have heard them in the past and thus will not be "prepped" to answer them.

Discount Their Comments

The comments that references make should be discounted on the basis that their names were provided by advisors who never knowingly provide bad references. You might ask: why even call them? Good question. The answer is that it might make you "feel" more comfortable with the advisor.

Performance Reports

A quality advisor provides investors with quarterly performance reports. Ask to see the reports of five clients that have been with the professional the longest. The advisor should delete the names to protect their identities. You can determine the longevity of the client relationship from the "since inception" date that is printed in the reports.

Advisor Insurance

All advisors should have adequate insurance to protect them from client claims. The insurance can be particularly important when independent advisors or small financial services companies provide advice on what to do with your assets.

Insured Risks

Your due diligence should require the disclosure of the advisors' insurance policies and a description of what exactly is covered under the policies. A common form of insurance is referred to as "errors and omissions." Taken at face value, the policy covers intentional as well as unintentional "mistakes" that damage you. In addition, there are others types of policies that protect the financial services firms from investor claims—you want to know what they are.

The Deductible

Insurance companies have begun raising deductibles from $10,000 and $25,000 to $100,000 and $250,000 for companies and professionals who service large amounts of assets. It is important for you to know that the company and the professional have the financial resources to pay the deductibles.

Bonding

Employees of the company or advisor will also have access to your financial data. It is important that all staff with access to account data be properly bonded with adequate amounts of coverage. Ask the advisor to provide information that documents the insurance companies and amounts.

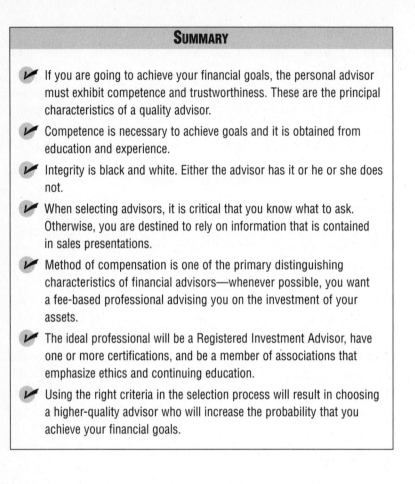

SUMMARY

✔ If you are going to achieve your financial goals, the personal advisor must exhibit competence and trustworthiness. These are the principal characteristics of a quality advisor.

✔ Competence is necessary to achieve goals and it is obtained from education and experience.

✔ Integrity is black and white. Either the advisor has it or he or she does not.

✔ When selecting advisors, it is critical that you know what to ask. Otherwise, you are destined to rely on information that is contained in sales presentations.

✔ Method of compensation is one of the primary distinguishing characteristics of financial advisors—whenever possible, you want a fee-based professional advising you on the investment of your assets.

✔ The ideal professional will be a Registered Investment Advisor, have one or more certifications, and be a member of associations that emphasize ethics and continuing education.

✔ Using the right criteria in the selection process will result in choosing a higher-quality advisor who will increase the probability that you achieve your financial goals.

6

DUE DILIGENCE

When it comes to your financial future, selecting the right professional to be your advisor is the most important decision you will ever make. A quality choice will produce more assets for your retirement years and more financial security late in life. A bad choice will result in fewer assets and less security. It is that simple, and it is that dramatic.

Once you know what to look for in an advisor, the process that you use to make your decision will determine the outcome. An objective process designed to obtain critical information about the competence and integrity of an advisor increases the odds of your making the right choice. What you need is a process that puts you in control of the information provided by the advisor candidates. Control is the vital ingredient—it increases your chances of hiring a quality advisor for the right reasons. This process is called due diligence.

A Process of Exclusion

Hiring a personal advisor is a process of exclusion. You can obtain initial information from six to eight advisors, review it, and reduce the number to four professionals. After you interview the four advisors, you select two finalists. After a second round of interviews, you select the one with the best qualifications.

The 4:2:1 process eliminates the three weakest advisors. You may exclude professionals due to deficiencies in their backgrounds, knowledge, integrity, combined expense structures, compensation, conflicts of interest, or other reasons.

Top Criteria and Ratings

The easiest way to implement a process of exclusion is to identify your top criteria for selecting an advisor—call it your top ten list. It describes what is most important to you when selecting an advisor. You may put a lot of emphasis on formal education, whereas another investor puts more importance on investment experience. Trustworthiness is one criterion that should always be on your top ten list.

Once you have identified your top criteria, you should enter them into a spreadsheet. It is much easier to compare advisor information when it is displayed side by side. You should also consider developing a rating system. Instead of writing down a lot of information, you can simply use a numeric range, such as 1 to 5. For example, a graduate degree from a quality school might rate a five, an undergraduate degree from a good school a three, and no degree a one.

You can also weight the value of each criterion. For example, you could weight the score for experience higher than the score for education. The advisors' compliance records might be weighted more than expense ratios, reflecting the importance of trust in the relationship.

This objective selection process is easy. Add up the ratings and select the professional with the highest score.

The Due Diligence Process

To make quality selections, you must have a structured process which you can diligently apply to every prospective advisor. The alternative is an unstructured process controlled by advisors—a very dangerous proposition considering that your financial future is at stake.

A structured due diligence process puts you in control of the advisor selection data. Control is critical, because with it you can obtain all of the vital information before you select a particular advisor who will influence your investments.

Subjectivity Versus Objectivity

Your goal must be to minimize the subjectivity of the selection process and maximize the objectivity. Stick with the subjective approach and, based upon our research, there is a greater than 75 percent probability that you will select an incompetent advisor. What is worse is that, if you are like most investors, you will end up repeating the process every few years when you replace the advisor, and suffer the consequences later in life when you run out of the time needed for accumulating adequate assets.

A completely objective evaluation process, however, increases the probability of achieving your financial goals. This process helps you identify, evaluate, and select advisors in the top 25 percent of the field who are competent and have integrity.

You Control the Data

It is essential that you control the information provided by advisors. When advisors control it, you risk being the recipient of carefully crafted presentations designed to make these individuals look as good as possible. You will only hear what they want you to hear.

When you control all of the information, you also receive standardized responses from advisors. This makes it much easier for you to compare their responses and apply your exclusion process. Comparisons are more difficult when you use different sales presentations as your primary source of input.

Structured Interviews

Structured interviews are important for the same reason. They enable you to compare the advisors' individual responses. To create consistency, you will have to provide each advisor with an identical agenda, set of questions, and timeline.

After reviewing the advisors' information and reducing the contenders to four, you should conduct two rounds of interviews. The purpose of the first round is to reduce the number of advisors down to the finalists who are interviewed in the second round. There may be four advisors in the first round and two in the second round of interviews. The second round also provides you with the opportunity to check first impressions before making a final decision.

Selecting a Winner

There is only one winner when you select a personal financial advisor. That individual becomes the consultant, coordinator, and gatekeeper for your assets. Do not confuse this person with money managers. Your advisor helps you select multiple managers to diversify your assets and minimize risk.

Finding Quality Advisors

There are only two ways to make initial contact with financial advisors: either you find them or they find you. There is no question that selecting advisors from those who find you is easier than finding your own. However, with convenience comes an extra element of risk. Sales-oriented advisors are the most active marketers, so they are the professionals who find you most frequently.

Advisors Who Find You

Most advisors actively market their services to you. It is how they grow their clientele and assets. Newer advisors, sales-oriented advisors, and advisors with smaller numbers of clients are the most active marketers. They need your assets more than fee-based advisors who are better established.

These advisors use a variety of strategies to create contact with you. They use direct mail, telemarketing, seminars, association memberships, and other techniques that put them in contact with investors. You probably do not appreciate some of their solicitation efforts, but it works for them. They are often able to build a sufficient client base through these efforts. However, you should never limit your search to advisors who find you.

You Find the Advisors

There are obvious benefits to finding the advisor yourself. First and foremost, you are not limited to hiring an advisor from the ones who solicited your business. Again, there is a high probability that the professionals who solicit are not the ones you want controlling your financial future. You can also choose the firm, location, and characteristics of the advisor when you are in control. You must have the personal discipline to keep looking until you find an advisor who has sufficient competence to help you achieve your goals. You need a strategy for finding high-quality advisors.

Referrals

Most quality advisors work on referral from current clients or other professionals, so the easiest way to find a quality advisor is to ask people whom you know and respect. Who would they recommend as investment professionals? Keep in mind that CPAs and attorneys are entering the financial services business, so they may refer you to an in-house professional. This is a biased referral, but the person still may represent a better choice than an advisor who finds you.

Referrals are not a substitute for due diligence; they are simply a relatively easy way to find advisors. Regardless of who introduced you to the advisor, you must still complete your own evaluation process. After all, the professional could be a friend of the referral source, and may not necessarily have the qualifications to be your advisor.

The Yellow Pages

The Yellow Pages may not sound desirable at first, but remember that you are the one doing the looking. Your selection is therefore not limited to those advisors who find you. You may discover that, after talking to disappointing referrals, the easiest process for finding professionals is a public list such as is found in the Yellow Pages.

However, finding the local phone number for Acme Financial Advisors does not solve the selection problem when the office employs 25 professionals. There will be a substantial range in the quality of advisors—very experienced to inexperienced, well educated to less educated, and great integrity to a lack of integrity. Which advisor do you choose?

One solution to this dilemma is to send a description of your requirements to the manager of the office. The manager will forward your information to the professionals in the office who meet your selection criteria. You may also want to limit the responses to the top five. To be safe, you should always interview professionals from different firms.

There is one caveat that bears mentioning should you decide to send your information to the branch manager. Some managers also work with clients, so they may try to keep the relationship for themselves. They also may send the documents to the "advisor of the day," the individual designated to receive all new leads on a given day. This is why you should ask for multiple responses and never deviate from the due diligence process.

Associations

Another strategy for finding a quality advisor is to contact national associations and obtain the names of the professionals in your area. All associations maintain websites with this information. Two of the better associations are the Investment Management Consultants Association and the Financial Planning Association.

You can obtain names from their websites or over the telephone and initiate the due diligence process. Do not make any assumptions about the significance of advisors' appearing on association websites. All members, regardless of competence or integrity, can be listed.

Websites

Several websites act as matchmakers between investors and professionals. Their primary purpose is to help you find advisors and provide some basic information about them. Then it is up to you to complete the necessary evaluation prior to selecting an advisor. It is imperative that you proceed with extreme caution when using this type of service for finding advisors. Websites make the process fast and convenient, but they also represent substantial risk for your financial future. You want to know who owns the sites in question, how they are connected to the advisors, whether they have any conflicts of interest, and how they are compensated. In other words, you want full disclosure if you are going to rely on websites to find advisors.

Assume that a particular website is a service which generates leads for advisors who are employed by the company that owns the site.

Any of their advisors can post information on this company-owned website.

Another site could be owned by a company that considers this a secondary service and is designed to produce traffic for their website. In this way, they can advertise other products and services.

There are also a few sites whose primary customers are investors rather than advisors. These sites provide a valuable service, but there should still be full disclosure about their ownership, conflicts of interest, and sources of compensation.

Do not let brand names on websites lull you into a false sense of security—you still have to do your homework to make sure that they have placed your interests ahead of their own. As long as you conduct your own due diligence, web-based referral programs are a good way to find advisors and to remain anonymous until you are ready to meet them.

The RFI Process

The most important element in your search for an advisor with high competence and integrity is the use of a formal Request For Information (RFI). The purpose of this document is to obtain pertinent information about advisors that you can use for evaluation and selection purposes.

You send the RFI to all of the professionals whom you are considering for the role of your personal advisor. There are no exceptions, not even if you know the advisors, consider them friends, or were referred to them by someone you trust. You should have all advisors complete the RFI in its entirety and provide it to you by a specified deadline.

Your financial future is too important to select an advisor any other way.

Boxes Versus Narrative

You want to make it easy for advisors to respond to your RFI and easy for you to review their responses. Therefore, all questions should have answers that require a checked response by the advisors. There are four reasons to limit responses to checkmarks:

1. Advisors will respond more quickly because it will take less time than narratives.
2. You can evaluate the responses faster.
3. Narratives introduce the possibility for sales information to be inserted into the responses.
4. It is easier to compare responses.

Objective Data Gathering

The RFI process provides you with a standard set of objective data for each advisor; these data are not influenced by the advisor's sales skills. If you obtain similar information in sales presentations, professionals will often modify their answers based on their perceptions of your needs and priorities. The modifications can be the application of their consulting skills, but more often, sales skills are used to influence your decisions. This reintroduces subjectivity into your selection process.

Identify Weaknesses

There is an unwritten rule in sales that presentations are designed to maximize strengths and minimize weaknesses. In fact, experienced advisors will never disclose information that may exclude them from your selection process. It is up to you to ask questions that uncover weaknesses. Therefore, one of the primary purposes of the RFI is to identify reasons not to select a particular advisor.

Advisor Reaction

Highly qualified professionals will welcome the opportunity to describe their credentials to you. They are justifiably proud of their accomplishments and realize that you need information to make your decisions.

Conversely, less qualified professionals who rely on sales skills to win your assets will resist your RFI because their credentials are not competitive. Their only options in this process are to try to talk you out of the need for an RFI, lie, or withdraw. If certain professionals try talking you out of providing the information, then you must assume they have something to hide, even if you like them. If they had nothing to hide, they would not resist answering the questions.

Requested Information

RFI data is important because it helps you form your initial impressions of advisors. These impressions are part of the process that you use for screening advisors and determining who makes it to the next level. Some answers to your RFI questions are more important than others. Consider them the short form version of due diligence. These critical elements focus on determining the competence and integrity of advisors. For example, education and experience are two critical elements because they directly impact the knowledge levels of the advisors. Compliance data are critical because they reflect the integrity of the advisor.

Work Experience

Work experience is one of two principal ways in which advisors build their knowledge base. You want complete disclosure about experience that is both related and unrelated to the financial services industry.

Education

The other way to acquire knowledge is through education. This includes college, continuing education, participation in seminars, certification programs, association memberships, and other programs that increase the knowledge bases of advisors.

Compliance Record

Integrity is even more important than knowledge. What is the value of knowledgeable professionals if you cannot trust their advice? Several of your RFI questions should focus on obtaining the information you need to evaluate the integrity of advisors.

Client complaints, regulatory problems, and criminal proceedings are just a few of the many topics that are included in this section of an RFI. As shocking as it may sound to you, individuals may have felony convictions and still obtain securities licenses—as long as the conviction did not include securities violations.

According to legal experts, 86 percent of investor lawsuits are without merit. The suits are initiated by upset investors who try to recover losses and have little or nothing to do with the integrity of the advisor. Unfortunately, they can still leave a blemish on the record of the advisor. You should be aware of them, but not use them as a reason to exclude an advisor from your selection process.

Compensation

Complete disclosure of compensation is a critical component of the RFI. You want to know every penny of compensation that you will produce for the various service providers in advance so you can determine their relative value. You must ask for the compensation of advisors, because they have no regulatory requirements to disclose the information to you. The greater the integrity of the advisor, the more forthcoming he or she will be with the information.

Advisor Services

You also should ask for a description of the services that are provided by the advisor. Are the services consulting, planning, both, or some other type of service? In addition, what types of clients does the advisor prefer to work with? The responses should also include number of clients and minimum asset amounts.

Hedge Words

Another reason to use checkboxes for responses is to minimize the advisors' use of hedge words. Some of these words are required by the regulators to make disclosures more accurate, but more often, they are used to change the meaning of responses.

Consider this example using the word "believe." One advisor states, "I have the skills to help you achieve your financial goals." Another advisor states, "I believe I have the skills to help you achieve your financial goals." The latter has hedged the response in case his or her skill sets are inadequate. Which advisor would you prefer for your assets? Additional examples of frequently used hedge words are provided in Chapter Four.

Disclosure Documents

Disclosure documents are attached to each RFI that the advisor must complete and sign. The disclosures cover a number of different topics:

- Compliance record
- Total compensation from all sources
- Statement of ethics
- Statement of knowledge
- Conflicts of interest
- References

The RFI Response

You should send your RFI to all of the professionals you are considering for the role of your personal financial advisor. Advisors normally do their best when they are competing to win your assets. If advisors are not responsive when they are trying to win your assets, what will they be like to work with after you select them? You can use the RFI response process as a tool for evaluating future service quality. Did you receive the RFIs by the deadline? Was all of the information provided as requested? Did the advisors try to modify any of the questions or responses?

Timeliness

You should give the advisors five to ten business days to complete the RFI on the basis that their actual time commitment is one hour or less. There is nothing in the RFI that will require advisors to do any extensive data gathering. In fact, the information should be readily available because other investors should have requested the same information.

You should be sensitive to advisors who may require extensions for one reason or another: vacation, illness, or extended meetings away from their offices. However, the advisor or an assistant should request the extension during the initial few days of the prescribed time period. It should not become an excuse for late responses.

Written Responses Only

Ideally, you will e-mail the RFI to advisors and request that they respond by e-mail. If that is not possible, you can fax or mail them a printed copy and have them respond accordingly. Regardless of how

RFIs are sent to advisors, it is mandatory that their responses be in writing, and signed off on as complete and accurate. Written responses are an extremely important component of your due diligence process, because professionals with something to hide will not like written disclosure. Once the RFI is in writing and in your possession, they have lost control over the distribution of the information. For all they know, you may forward their information to superiors, compliance officers, or regulatory agencies.

Inferior advisors prefer the relative safety of verbal communications. If anything goes wrong in the relationship, they are in a better position to deny having made particular statements—it is your word against theirs, and you can safely assume that these advisors only remember details that benefit them. They have no defense when their representations are in writing, because they have signed the document as being true and accurate.

Overall Strength

Advisors must be judged on the overall quality of their responses, because each will have strengths and weaknesses. You may find the perfect advisor with no visible weaknesses, which will make your selection decision easy. However, you should be prepared to add up an advisor's strong points and deduct the individual's weak points to tally overall strength. Doing so for each potential advisor will enable you to select your eventual winner.

Low-Quality Responses

Some advisors will make half-hearted efforts to complete the RFI, because they view it as additional work and reason that they have a low probability of winning. If they do not win, there is no way for them to get paid. You should not be concerned about these types of professionals because they are usually the more sales-oriented ones you would not want as your advisor in the first place. They have done you a favor by excluding themselves.

Higher-quality advisors are used to RFIs, however, and use them to gather information on money managers and other types of service providers whom they recommend for your assets.

The Disclaimers

Similar to hedge words, disclaimers may be included in your RFI responses that change the meaning of the information. It is imperative that you read these disclaimers and ascertain how they affect the information you are reviewing. Some of the more important disclaimers are attached to credentials, investment proposals, risk levels, and compliance records.

The Non-Response

You must assume that advisors who refuse to answer particular questions have something to hide. They may put "n/a" (not available) or "confidential" in the space you provide for the response. They may have a valid reason for not providing it; however, there is a higher probability that the information is available, but it is negative and will detract from the impressions that advisors are trying to create.

There is an easy way to make this determination. For example, you send RFIs to four advisors; three respond to all of your questions, and one does not. This tells you that the information in question is available and is not confidential. One of the four does not want to provide the information for some reason, but it does not matter—simply exclude this advisor from further consideration in your selection process.

As Advertised

Advisors want you to select them based on their sales presentations. This is the equivalent of buying a car after seeing it advertised in the newspaper. It is not how you buy cars. Instead, you test drive cars, talk to experts, read third party evaluations, and compare the vehicles to their competition—feature for feature and dollar for dollar. You want to make a good decision, because you will depend on the car for reliable transportation over the next several years. You should do the same amount of research with advisors. Make sure they are as good as advertised.

Statement of Accuracy

Part of the RFI process is to require advisors to sign a statement which you developed stating that all of their responses are true, accurate, and not subject to any qualifications.

Your Personal Profile

The next step in the due diligence process is the development of a personal profile that prospective advisors will use to get to know you and your financial requirements. They will use this information to determine if there is a fit and to develop their investment proposals. The profile also enables you to communicate consistent information to the advisors. This way, they are all using the same information, and it is easier for you to evaluate their responses.

Your Information

Your profile is a comprehensive description of your personal and financial situation. You will need to provide the following information if you want the advisors to develop a quality investment proposal:

- Personal information about you and your family, such as ages, college plans for children, anticipated retirement dates, tax rates, health, anticipated longevity, etc.
- Your current financial situation. Include all of your various investment accounts, their balances, and how the assets are currently invested.
- All sources and amounts of current income and anticipated increases in that income until retirement. If you are currently retired, provide the same information to age 90.
- Your total living expenses, current debt, and how you expect those amounts to change over time.
- Your strategies for accumulating assets: savings rates and amounts, inheritance, stock option programs, retirement plans, bonuses, etc.
- Your plans for spending your current and future assets: major purchases, college educations for your children, and retirement are the predominant ones.
- Your current investment goals, tolerance for risk, and any preferences that will impact the proposals of prospective advisors. For example, your requirement may be for domestic investments or 50 percent fixed income.
- Your expectations and tolerances for the management of your assets.

- Any preferences, restrictions, or concerns in regard to the investment of your assets.

Do not provide this information to advisors until after you have screened their responses to your RFI. There is no reason to provide personal data to excluded advisors.

Expectations and Tolerances

Your personal profile must describe your performance and service expectations, as well as your tolerance for risk. Think about the amount of assets that you will need in order to achieve all of your financial goals and the amount of risk you are willing to take to achieve these goals. The advisors' strategies must describe how they are going to produce the desired asset amounts within your tolerance for risk.

Determine the amount of assets you will need when you retire, then deduct current assets as well as the amounts you can realistically save between now and your retirement date. The advisors can convert the time and asset amounts into average rates of return to calculate your performance requirements.

Providing your risk tolerance is crucial so your advisor candidates can propose realistic investment strategies. One way to view risk is to determine the percentage of your assets that are invested in the stock market. For example, if you are an all-equity investor in your thirties, you should expect periodic down years of 15 percent or more. Conservative investors expose their assets to less risk by owning less volatile stocks and a higher percentage of bonds or other asset classes, such as income-producing real estate.

Your expectations and tolerances must be reasonable so that your goals have high probabilities of occurring. Exceptionally high assumptions may sound good, but if the returns fail to materialize, you will have a significant shortfall, which could result in deferred retirement or a reduced standard of living.

Preferences, Restrictions, and Concerns

You should also include your preferences, restrictions, and concerns in your profile. This very important information enables prospective advisors to customize their investment proposals for your assets.

Preferences are what you would like to see happen with your assets. For example, you might prefer domestic investments, moderate risk, and tax-efficient portfolios. The advisors must know all of your preferences before they can recommend appropriate solutions.

Restrictions are what you do not want to see in your portfolio. For example, you might not want alcohol, tobacco, nuclear, or gambling stock investments. Other examples of restrictions are never to take net short-term capital gains in your portfolio or not to buy a particular company's stock because you are an employee of that company.

Whereas preferences and restrictions are specific and fact-based, concerns reflect your emotional involvement with your assets and the investment process. For example, you might be so concerned about sizeable losses that, to avoid them, you are willing to forgo the potential for substantial gains. This may be an irrational concern, but for you, it is real. This is critical information for prospective advisors.

The Interviews

The next process is the initial interview, which also serves as an additional data-gathering and screening step. Advisors who make it through this step are your finalists.

The interview should be the easiest step for you, because you are used to talking to advisors. It is how you selected them in the past. The principal difference now is that you are in control of the information that is provided during the interview.

The Agenda

You control all interviews by providing prospective advisors with an agenda that describes the information you want covered. This accomplishes three goals. First, like the RFI, you obtain the information you need to complete this step of the selection process; second, you can compare the advisors information more easily; and third, you minimize the impact of their sales skills and focus on investment knowledge, integrity, and proposed strategy.

The 40-Minute Interview

You want to limit the amount of time that a professional has to present credentials and convince you that he or she should be your advisor. After all, you already have a substantial amount of information provided by their RFI responses. The purpose of the 40-minute presentation is not to listen to a repeat of the same information. A rigid timeline also minimizes the impact of advisors' sales skills and makes them focus on information that is important to you.

You want the opportunity to meet with prospective advisors for four principal reasons:

1. Determine if you would be comfortable working with their personality types for the next several years—the only subjective evaluation in the selection process.
2. Determine how they will add value that justifies the compensation you will be paying them.
3. Determine how they differentiate themselves from their competition.
4. Review their proposed strategy and investment policy for your assets.

Twenty Minutes for Questions and Answers

Allow a maximum of twenty minutes for questions and answers (Q&A) immediately after the presentations. You must ask questions that will help you make your decisions. The answers will determine the winner in close races.

It is important that you do not distribute your questions in advance. This forces the advisors to think on their feet and lets you see a different side of the professionals that you never see when they have time to prepare presentations or responses.

There are two types of questions. Some questions are prepared in advance so you can focus on listening to advisors' responses rather than thinking about your next question. Other questions occur to you during the presentations.

The most important questions to ask advisors, however, always relate to your personal situation:

- How would they describe appropriate goals for someone with your profile?
- Can they describe the investment strategy of one of their best clients who is similar to you?
- How would they describe their philosophy in regard to investment risk versus reward?
- Do they believe that active management and higher expenses are superior to passive management and lower expenses for certain asset classes? If yes, why?
- What is their market outlook, or their firm's, for the performance of various asset classes in the next few years?

The Proposed Strategy

Each prospective advisor should review the information in your personal profile and develop a proposed strategy for your assets. This may not be the actual strategy you implement with the advisor you select, but it is one more way to measure their competence and integrity. In addition, weak proposals will be easy to identify when they are compared to strong proposals. It is also an excellent way to compare advisors and their relative costs.

Proposed Strategies

Provide your profile to prospective advisors and ask them to develop an overall strategy tailored for your assets based on your current situation and goals for retirement. You should give all of them the same goal and time frame to work with—for example, planning to retire in 15 years—so you can more easily compare the proposals of multiple advisors.

As a cautionary note, remember that the professionals have the benefit of hindsight. They will no doubt select high-performing managers and allocations from the past when proposing future strategies. You must look beyond the performance data to determine the actual quality of their proposals.

Proposed Portfolio

Advisors' proposed investment strategies should include the following information:

- A description of your goals
- A description of your current strategy
- Current and proposed asset allocation models
- The proposed managers for your strategy
- The separate and blended track records of the proposed managers
- The total expense structure for their proposal
- Your exposure to current and future risk
- The relationship between the risk of their proposal and the return

Comparative Analysis

The prospective advisors can use the data you provided about your current portfolio along with their proposed portfolios to produce side-by-side comparisons that will make it easy for you to see their recommended changes. The comparison should include the following information:

- Their description of the weaknesses in your current portfolio
- Asset allocation by class and style of management
- Asset allocation by geography (domestic, international, and global)
- Performance for one-, three- and five-year time periods
- Risk analysis of the two portfolios
- Expense analysis of the two portfolios
- The tax consequences of liquidating your current portfolio
- The financial impact of the current and proposed portfolios on your assets for the next three, five, and ten years

Your purpose for requiring advisors to provide the comparison is to gain as much confidence as possible that their proposal is superior to your current investment strategy—in particular, if you have to pay taxes to liquidate your existing portfolio to implement their proposed strategy.

Manager Analysis Versus Benchmarks

You should also require that the advisors provide you with a comparison of their proposal to appropriate investment benchmarks. For example, one advisor might show you proposed manager A's track record compared to the performance of the S&P 500. Another one might show you proposed manager B's track record compared to the Russell 2000, and so on.

Next, the advisors should blend the returns of the proposed managers to produce combined returns. Then they should do the same thing with the benchmarks. The blended returns show you how all of your assets are performing versus the combined returns of the benchmarks, which reflect the performance of all of the market segments.

Once again, you want some assurance that the advisors' proposed portfolios can beat the markets net of their expenses.

Features and Benefits

Advisor proposals should also include a summary description of unique features and benefits of their recommended investment strategy. You should not have to deduce them on your own. For example, if a proposal reduces risk (the benefit), you want to know how it does this (the feature). If a proposal minimizes your taxes, you want the details of how this is accomplished. You also want to know the probability of occurrence for the proposal.

The Winner

The advisor who produces the best proposal with the maximum number of benefits, the fewest negatives, and the highest probability of achievement should be given serious consideration as the winner. The ultimate benefit is attaining the assets you need for a financially secure future.

The Hiring Decision

You have reviewed all of the advisors' information contained in their RFIs, interviewed the four finalists, and eliminated two of the potential candidates from consideration. Now it is time to make the final decision. You may find it more difficult than you thought—especially if your semifinalists are relatively identical.

Quality Looks Alike

At some point in the selection process, you may begin to think that all advisors look and sound alike. They are well educated, have substantial experience, a history of high integrity, and they all have good ideas that will help you achieve your financial goals. The better your screening process, the more likely it is this will be true. Your challenge is to identify and evaluate the unique strengths and weaknesses of each advisor. These characteristics offset each other, which makes your decision more difficult.

Objectivity Turns to Subjectivity

You must maintain your objectivity at least until you reach the last step and you have identified the final two candidates. Then, assuming both candidates have similar qualities, you should pick the one you like the best. Going with your feelings at the very end of the selection process is acceptable because you have been objective up to that point.

Balanced Decision

In the final analysis, you want to make a balanced decision that takes into account all of the information you have collected in the RFI and interview processes. The need for balance addresses a multitude of issues—for example, higher returns versus lower expenses and higher levels of personal service versus better quality reporting.

You risk a bad decision when you overweight certain criteria. For example, you might put excessive importance on a proposal that displays higher results, even though you know that performance is difficult to reproduce. Advisors who overweight results are doing you a major disservice. Their goal is to appeal to your greed and hope that you ignore other criteria that paint a much more realistic picture.

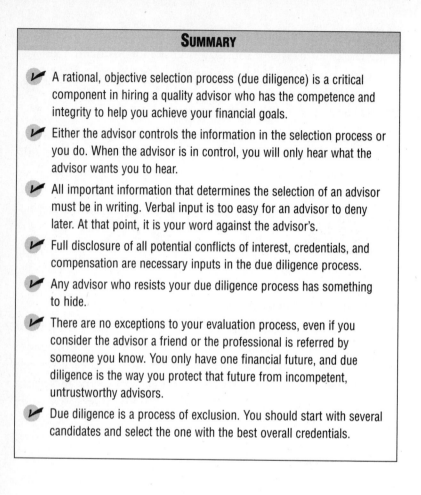

SUMMARY

✔ A rational, objective selection process (due diligence) is a critical component in hiring a quality advisor who has the competence and integrity to help you achieve your financial goals.

✔ Either the advisor controls the information in the selection process or you do. When the advisor is in control, you will only hear what the advisor wants you to hear.

✔ All important information that determines the selection of an advisor must be in writing. Verbal input is too easy for an advisor to deny later. At that point, it is your word against the advisor's.

✔ Full disclosure of all potential conflicts of interest, credentials, and compensation are necessary inputs in the due diligence process.

✔ Any advisor who resists your due diligence process has something to hide.

✔ There are no exceptions to your evaluation process, even if you consider the advisor a friend or the professional is referred by someone you know. You only have one financial future, and due diligence is the way you protect that future from incompetent, untrustworthy advisors.

✔ Due diligence is a process of exclusion. You should start with several candidates and select the one with the best overall credentials.

7

CONSULTANTS

The financial services industry is in the early stages of transforming. It is moving from selling investment products for commissions to providing value-added advice for fees. This is a slow process, but eventually it will cause the industry to be comprised of investor-friendly companies and professionals whose principal focus is the achievement of your financial goals.

The advisors for this new business model are called financial consultants. Based on our research, less than twenty-five percent of all professionals have transitioned all or even a portion of their clients to the new model. The top five percent are pure consultants, while the other 20 percent are in transition from commission to fee, so they do both.

It is important to note the advisors who made the transition to consulting almost to a person did so on their own initiative and not due to a mandate from their companies. In effect, they personally determined that consulting was the level of service most investors needed to achieve their financial goals—the other alternative was to continue to sell products for commissions. Their personal initiative has raised the standards of the industry and is one more reason why they are the advisor-type of choice for millions of investors.

Investment Knowledge

One of the reasons that there are so few very high-quality consultants (less than five percent of the 650,000 licensed professionals) is that a substantial amount of knowledge is required. It is an unfortunate reality, however, that the industry is willing to spend more money on sales skills than on investment knowledge. The result is that only a small percentage of all advisors can legitimately call themselves financial consultants.

Most advisors have nominal knowledge and advanced selling skills. Consequently, there is a marked difference between sales-oriented advisors and advice-oriented consultants. Consultants are in the knowledge business and the more they know, the better job they can do for your assets. This better job translates into hundreds of thousands of additional dollars for your retirement and increased financial security late in life.

This chapter describes the core competencies, services, and characteristics of consultants, so you will be able to recognize the qualities when you evaluate them. In addition, if you have ever thought that the fee you pay for financial advice is too high, wait until you read about the knowledge that real consultants must have and the high value-added services they provide.

Core Competencies

Consultants are your link to the money management firms that make investment decisions for securities. Their role is critical if you do not have the time or expertise to personally manage your own assets or to select quality decision makers like separate account, mutual fund, and hedge fund managers.

The performance of your assets is largely determined by the quality of the consultant whom you select to help you. This professional provides the primary input you will rely on to make important decisions for your financial future—for example, asset allocation, manager selection, and risk management. You will learn to rely on these services because you have to—the consultant is the expert.

Predicting the Future

Consultants must understand economics, but this does not mean that the professional will be able to predict GDP growth, inflation, or interest rates. Even the most sophisticated econometric modeling systems in the world cannot make these predictions with any consistent degree of accuracy.

Periodically you read about a professional who predicted a downturn in the economy or an industry group. This does not mean that the person is a genius or knows something no one else knows. There are simply too many variables. There is a high probability that it was luck—when thousands of economists make predictions, someone is bound to be right.

You should not expect your consultants to predict the future. In fact, if they try to, you should see it as a red flag. Instead, your consultant should be skilled at developing strategies that work in a variety of economic conditions.

Financial Goal Setting

You should develop your own personal goals such as choosing a retirement date and determining an income requirement. Then it is up to your consultant to help you convert personal goals into financial goals. For example, your goal might be to retire at age 65 with an annual income of $84,000 per year to maintain your current standard of living. To turn this into a reality, your consultant will help you make several critical decisions that include the following:

- The amount of assets you will need to meet your income requirement
- The returns you will need to achieve your asset goals
- The amount of risk you will have to incur to achieve your goals
- The allocation of assets that will achieve your goals
- The returns you will need to protect the purchasing power of your assets after retirement

It is important that you establish realistic goals; otherwise, all subsequent steps in the investment process are tainted. For example, there is no investment strategy that has a high probability of producing 20 percent returns year in and year out. Although this is a financial goal, it is not an attainable one.

Establishing realistic financial goals that have a high probability of occurring is a complex process that requires substantial knowledge and experience. For example, you may have unrealistically high performance expectations, prompting you to rationalize saving less. If the actual performance is less than expected, though, you will have fewer assets to fund a comfortable, safe retirement. Unrealistic expectations can compromise your ability to achieve your goals.

The development of realistic goals is critical because they are the foundation of your investment strategy. The higher the goals, the more risk you have to take when investing your assets. As a general rule, higher goals increase the probability of failure and lower goals increase the probability of success.

Financial Strategy

Developing a financial strategy is also a complex process that requires specialized consulting skills. In its most basic form, a strategy is your game plan for achieving your goals. It is the roadmap for your financial future that includes:

- How assets are allocated between classes
- Who manages the assets
- Who holds the asset in custody
- How risk is managed
- What restrictions apply to investments
- What are the geographical limitations for investments
- What are the income requirements
- What are the net asset flows to the managers

Investment Policy

Once the strategy has been finalized, it is important that your consultant know how to document it with a written Investment Policy Statement (IPS). An IPS is a document that outlines your financial goals, the strategy for achieving them, your asset allocation, the manager for each asset class, restrictions, and other important information. Its primary purpose is to minimize the risk of miscommunication between you, your consultant, and the money managers. Your future financial security is too important to be based on verbal instructions. The IPS makes sure that all of your service providers are on the same page.

Investment Horizon

Horizon is a frequently misunderstood term; it is best defined as the amount of time that passes before you need your assets or income from the assets. It is also an important input for determining your tolerance for risk. Short horizons have lower tolerances, because you have less time to recover from bad years. Long horizons are just the opposite. You may also have multiple horizons based on a variety of potential needs. For example, if the current year is 2003 and you are 40 years old:

- The accumulation of assets to build a second home in 2008 would have a five-year horizon.
- The accumulation of assets to send your children to college beginning in 2012 would have a nine-year horizon.
- Income distributions from your accumulated assets when you retire in 2028 have a 25-year horizon followed by an additional 25-year horizon for your retirement years.

Asset Allocation

Many consultants believe that allocation is the most important investment decision you will make for your assets. In fact, a now-famous study by Brinson, Hood, and Beebower concluded that 93.6 percent of performance results from the allocation of assets. Think of allocation as "being in the right place at the right time with your assets." For example, you own a high percentage of stocks when the equity markets are positive and a low percentage when they are negative. The report states that being invested in the market at the right time is more important than which stocks you own.

The same is true when allocating assets between stocks and bonds. If your allocations are wrong, it does not matter who is managing your assets—your performance will suffer regardless. If the stock market declines 25 percent and 80 percent of your assets are invested in the equity market, your investments will incur a significant loss in market value.

Because the perfect allocation is impossible to predict in advance, consultants always recommend diversification, so that at least a portion of your assets are in the right place at the right time. This is a complex process which requires a significant amount of knowledge and specialized software for developing an optimized allocation based on your return objective and tolerance for risk.

For these reasons, your advisor should be very knowledgeable about alternative allocation strategies and their impact on the performance and risk exposure of your assets.

Money Manager Selection

Manager research, the foundation of the manager selection process, is a vital service that is not usually conducted by the consultant. Due to the time-consuming nature of the evaluations, consultants have specialized support staff members that analyze money management firms. By delegating work to other professionals, your advisor has more time to spend with you.

Multiple Managers

You have $300,000 and decide to invest with one manager who invests in multiple asset classes. However, this is not the strategy you would receive from your consultant. Most often, the professional will recommend multiple managers who specialize in investing in particular asset classes, styles, and geographies. Therefore, it is imperative that your advisor knows how to structure investment strategies that utilize several managers to maximize performance and minimize risk.

Risk Management

The most commonly used indicator of risk is the volatility of the securities markets. That is, markets go up and down based on a large number of unpredictable variables, including the economy, company results, and investor sentiment. Investments with large price swings are considered more volatile (riskier) than investments with small price swings. For example, a technology stock that sold for $140 per share at its peak is now selling for $5 a share. This is extraordinary volatility. Now compare these price swings to those of a utility stock that trades between $30 and $50 per share. Here, the utility stock is much less risky than the tech stock. Of course, there is a substantial difference between the two stocks in terms of upside potential.

Your ultimate risk is not the volatility of the securities markets; it is the potential failure of not achieving your financial goals. In fact, you should not even be concerned about the ups and downs of the markets as long as you are confident that you will be able to accumulate and preserve an adequate amount of assets. This requires realistic goals, a smart strategy, a long-term investment horizon, and quality managers to make the day-to-day decisions. In other words, it is critical that your consultant know how to develop a risk-managed strategy for volatile markets.

Rebalancing

Rebalancing is the process of changing the current allocation of your assets back to the original allocation or, if your outlook for the future has changed, a new allocation. For example, your original allocation one year ago was 50 percent stocks and 50 percent bonds. Today, your allocation is 70 percent stocks and 30 percent bonds, because stocks outperformed bonds. Your risk exposure has increased because stocks are now overweighted and bonds are underweighted. Rebalancing is the service that brings allocations back into line with your tolerance for risk. Quality consultants provide this service on a quarterly, semiannual, and annual frequency depending on the tax effect.

Monitor Investments

You should never invest your assets with money managers and then ignore how they execute your strategy. This is a risky way to invest, because it assumes that everything will be as expected when just the opposite is more probable—everything in the investment world is subject to change. You and your consultant must adapt your strategy to these changes. It is the role of the consultant to monitor the money managers' investments as well as watch a substantial number of additional variables. Following are a few of the most important inputs:

- The managers' adherence to your investment policy
- The managers' investments in relation to their stated style of management
- Your exposure to risk by manager
- Absolute and relative investment performance
- Excessive cash positions
- Realized gains and losses
- The continuity of the manager's professional staff
- Allocations by asset class, geography, sector of the economy, and security

Reporting Performance

Quality consultants always provide a quarterly performance report that is an anaysis of your investments, allocations, cash flows, performance, and risk. The report is usually delivered personally by the consultant. The professional can then review results, discuss strategy, and answer any questions you may have. Performance reporting is the primary value-added, continuous service provided by consultants.

Replacing Managers

From time to time, it is necessary to replace a manager for any one of several reasons: several senior staff members may have left the firm, underperformance was experienced for several quarters, or there were unacceptable changes in the characteristics of the portfolio. It is the role of the consultant to recognize the problems as soon as possible and recommend action steps.

Money Managers

The most important consultant skill that will impact the future performance of your assets is the selection of high-quality money managers to make securities decisions. Quality managers produce higher returns over long time periods even though they may not always be the most successful short-term managers. For example, some managers have excellent five-year track records, but there are one-year periods during which they underperformed. The one-year lag occurs when their strategy is temporarily out of synch with the market. Your goal should be to win the war, not necessarily every battle, by picking the best managers for the long haul.

There is a proliferation of services on the Internet which lead you to believe that the selection of money managers is easy. "Just pick brand names with the highest track records," the services advise. Like market timing, this easy-sounding technique does not work. These services will convince you to select yesterday's winners when there is substantial evidence that most money managers have a difficult time repeating their successes.

Due Diligence and Money Managers

Just as you complete due diligence on advisors, consultants use the same process (albeit with different questions) for evaluating money managers. The selection of quality managers requires hours and hours of objective research that includes the evaluation of questionnaires, conference calls, onsite visitations, and painstaking attention to detail. Only a small percentage of managers have the credentials and resources to produce consistent results for your assets. Your consultants have to review a lot of data to find the best managers.

Good consultants always have a team of professionals supporting them. In a typical situation, members of the team complete the due diligence process and monitor the managers. The research process must be extremely thorough and not limited to managers' historical performance or marketing literature. For example, one popular evaluation methodology has more than 400 points of data that are evaluated and maintained for each manager by trained specialists. Then all of the data are updated quarterly. The quantity and frequency of data is why the consultant does not do this work solo.

This research process has two primary goals: to identify quality managers that have higher probabilities of delivering superior results in the future and to avoid lower quality managers that represent reduced returns and excessive risk. When you think about it, these are the same goals that you have in the advisor due diligence process. When these two goals are achieved, the probability of your realizing important financial objectives is greatly enhanced.

Track Records

Why conduct comprehensive due diligence when you could simply select the managers with the best track records? One reason is that past performance is not an accurate indicator of future performance. Here are a few additional reasons why:

- The securities markets are in a constant state of change with a variety of characteristics.
- Superior investment professionals frequently leave high-performing money management firms to leverage their success by starting their own firms. Their departure can undermine future performance.
- Success attracts too many assets. Excessive amounts of new assets can negatively impact the investment strategies of managers, thereby reducing future performance.
- Some managers drift away from the investment processes and styles that made them successful. They do this because they are seeking better performance in other asset classes and styles of management.

Performance records are the Pied Pipers of the investment world. They seemingly make selection simple, and they appeal to your innate desires for higher performance and quick, easy decisions. However, they are the tip of the iceberg. The most important information to obtain about managers is how they produced the record and whether or not they can produce superior returns in the future.

Tax-Efficient Investing

One of your consultant's core competencies should be to minimize the impact of taxes on your investment performance. Taxes are one of the primary forms of erosion because they reduce the amount of money you have for reinvestment. The process of minimizing taxes on investments is frequently referred to as tax-efficient investing. It has a broad range of meanings depending on the consultant and the money manager.

Real Tax Efficiency

There is an increasing awareness among investors that taxes are an expense that can be minimized with efficient investment strategies. However, money managers would rather not invest on a tax-efficient basis because it requires additional work. Since professional staff is the majority of their overhead, their profitability is reduced. The result is that many managers say they are tax-efficient but, in fact, do very little to minimize taxes. For example, they reduce their turnover rates or make sure that capital gains are long-term. However, up to 16 investment techniques minimize taxes on income and capital gains. Six of the common ones are:

1. Some stocks pay dividends and some do not. One way to minimize taxes is to buy stocks that pay little or no dividends.
2. Low turnover (sales) portfolios generate fewer taxable events than high turnover portfolios.
3. Offsetting taxable gains with losses will reduce your tax bill.
4. Harvesting losses late in the year, even if you buy the stocks back in January, will reduce your year-end tax bill.
5. There is no state income tax when you invest in government bonds.
6. There are no state or federal taxes when you invest in municipal bonds that are issued by your state of residence.

Certain strategies may be more applicable for investors in higher tax brackets. Regardless of your tax rate, your advisor should be able to design and implement investment strategies that minimize taxes. This service helps to cost justify the fee you pay them.

Gross and Net Performance

Investors are also becoming increasingly aware of the differences between gross and net performance. The sources of the differences are forms of erosion—primarily taxes and investment expenses. Some money managers will tell you that investment performance, risk management, and tax efficiency cannot be accomplished in the same portfolio. For example, one tax technique is to minimize turnover in your portfolios—in particular, selling that triggers net, short-term

capital gains. This may force managers to retain securities that they
would otherwise sell. Performance may be reduced, because they are
holding a security longer than they originally wanted to.

Investment "winners" may be held in concentrated positions, but
they should be thinned to reduce risk. Like all other investment
processes, there are pros and cons that your consultant should understand and be able to explain to you.

Discretion Is Liability

Most financial consultants and their companies go to great lengths to
avoid liability for their recommendations. Their principal strategy is
make you the decision maker and themselves the source of information and recommendations you must approve.

The Nondiscretionary Service Level

Consulting is viewed as a nondiscretionary service because the professionals do not make investment decisions. For example, when they provide background information on three money managers for an asset
class and you pick the one you like the best, you are the decision maker.

Recommendations and supporting information are not decisions.
When services are nondiscretionary, the person with the authority to
execute on their recommendations is the decision maker, and that
person is you.

The Discretionary Service Level

A form of consulting does include discretion for investment decisions, consequently, these professionals may not call themselves
consultants. Instead, they frequently describe their role as money
managers, because they make investment decisions on your behalf.
However, this title is a little misleading. They do not make the same
decisions as traditional money managers who select securities for your
portfolios. Instead, they continue to act as intermediaries, albeit discretionary intermediaries. Rather than picking securities, they have
the authority to select managers and allocate assets to them. They also
replace managers who are not meeting expectations. In addition, they
rebalance portfolios by reallocating assets between classes and man-

agers to reduce risk. All of these decisions are made without contacting you in advance. These professionals provide a discretionary level of service that is frequently called "manage the manager."

This is the highest level of service that is provided by advisors and requires an exceptional level of competence and integrity. You can also expect to pay a higher fee for this level of service.

The Fine Line

Just because advisors, firms, and their agreements say that they are providing nondiscretionary services does not mean the courts agree with this assertion. In fact, court decisions are beginning to label services discretionary on the basis that "influence is control."

Most consultants have extraordinary amounts of influence over investors. They make recommendations and investors follow them— often 100 percent of the time. After all, why would you second-guess a purported expert whose advice you are paying for? In legal matters, the debate centers around who the actual decision maker was. Was it the consultant, who controlled your choices by recommending a particular manager for an asset class? Or was it you, whose decision was based on the advice of professional? There is no handy, "across-the-board" answer, because there are too many variables. Be aware that this is not a black-and-white issue in the eyes of the court.

Compensation

There are three ways to compensate consultants for their services: fees, commissions, or some combination of the two. The best consultants are always compensated exclusively with fees and not with commissions that are the result of transactions or product sales. Very few consultants work for commissions, because they represent an out-of-date business model that has been dying a slow death for years.

Fee-Only

When consultants are referred to as *fee-only*, it means that their only method of compensation for their services is a fee. They do not accept any form of commission for these services. In fact, many consultants have allowed their securities licenses to lapse, so they could not accept commissions even if they wanted to. In lieu of licenses, they work exclusively under their RIA registration.

Fees are usually expressed as a percentage of the market value of your assets. For example, a one percent fee on $300,000 is $3,000. This is usually the only fee that consultants charge; however, some will charge additional fees for custom services, such as complex investment policies, asset allocation models, and manager searches, for they require additional hours of work.

Watch out for consultants who describe themselves as *fee-based* rather than fee-only. It could mean that they charge fees for some services and commissions for other services. At a minimum, though, they are reserving the right to charge a commission.

Wrap Fee

The fees of multiple service providers are frequently "wrapped" together and presented as one fee. Service providers can include the consultant, the consultant's company, money managers, and a custodian. There are no transaction-based fees of any kind when the consultant uses a wrap fee.

Wrap fees are desirable because they "fix" all of the expenses as a percentage of your assets, and they eliminate variable expenses, such as transaction costs. Another benefit of a wrap fee is that you always know what you are paying in advance. The fee may also be tax-deductible subject to certain limitations (consult your CPA).

The bad news about this type of fee, like all other fees, is that it can be excessive. This is why you want to interview multiple consultants and have them compete for your assets. The best proposal is the one with the highest level of service and the lowest cost.

Commission-Only

Before consultants were paid with fees, they were paid with commissions—a reflection of the industry's brokerage heritage. That is, they participated in the transaction charges that were generated by the managers' trading of securities in your portfolio. This practice created numerous conflicts of interest. For example, consultants recommended managers who produced high portfolio turnover and the resultant high commissions. Another technique for maximizing commissions was to recommend the frequent replacement of managers. The consultant made money when the former manager's portfolio was sold and the replacement manager's portfolio was purchased.

Fortunately, this method of compensation has just about gone the way of the dinosaur and is being rapidly replaced by asset-based fees. Never pay a consultant with commissions.

Fee-and-Commission

Fee-and-commission compensation should be considered a form of double dipping if the consultant participates in both. The most common form of this overcharging occurs when the professional charges a fee for advice and a commission for the purchase and sale of securities. The consultant can be paid a portion of the transaction charge with no disclosure requirements. If a brokerage firm has to pay commissions on transactions, it increase its charges to you. Simply put, you should not select consultants who charge both fees and commissions for their services.

Fixed Fees

Another type of consulting fee is fixed because some professionals have recognized that their primary variable for billing is time rather than your asset amount. As an example, a consultant charges a fee of $2,500 for an investment policy. The fee is a function of the number of hours it took to complete the policy multiplied by the professional's billing rate—ten hours at $250 per hour. An advisor might charge $10,000 for a manager search and $10,000 per year for performance reporting. Some charges are one-time fees such as for a manager search, while others are annual such as for performance reporting.

These billing arrangements are the same as the way you pay your attorney or CPA. In this case, the fixed fee is for specific value-added services and is a stark contrast to a fee that is a percentage of the market value of your asssets.

Conflicts of Interest

Consultants have the fewest conflicts when compared to other types of financial professionals because most consultants provide unrestricted choices, and their amount of compensation is not impacted by your investment decisions. These features of your relationship with a consultant eliminate most major sources of conflicts.

Investment Products

However, some consultants limit your choices because it improves their incomes and the profit margins of their companies. When this occurs, your advisor is not a consultant but rather a sales representative masquerading as a consultant. For this reason, it is critical that all consultants be required to disclose any product or compensation conflicts that result from their recommendations.

Fake Consultants

If an advisor determines that you want a consultant for your assets, this advisor may instantly become a consultant—whether or not the individual has the requisite skill set. The advisor will use this role and skillful sales techniques to win your assets. You should be aware that any professional can claim the job title of consultant because there are no clear standards or rules that regulate the roles of advisors. As a result, less scrupulous companies and advisors assume the role that the investor seems to want.

A serious conflict occurs when advisors misleadingly call themselves consultants to help win your trust and assets. You may believe that you are selecting an objective source of quality advice, while the relationship is actually based on a deceptive sales practice. This win-at-any-cost sales strategy also makes your selection decision more difficult; you have to be able to differentiate the real consultants from the charlatans.

The only way you can determine if you are dealing with a real consultant is to compare their services, characteristics, and compensation with the description of the ideal factors provided in this book. If there is a match, and the professional is willing to provide full disclosure, then you are evaluating a real consultant. If there is not a match, or the advisor resists certain disclosures, you should automatically exclude this individual from your selection process.

Favorite Managers

Some consultants place all of their clients' assets with particular money managers. This may be only a small issue if the managers are of exceptional quality. However, it is a major issue if they are not.

Limiting your choices to certain managers is always in conflict with your need for the best investment advice. For example, if a consultant has a personal relationship with a manager, or is paid additional compensation to recommend particular managers, you may be receiving a lower level of service due to his or her lack of objectivity. Some managers will even support the sales and service efforts of consultants by paying some of their expenses. Full disclosure, though, prevents this from happening with your assets.

The Cookie Cutter

Another potential conflict of interest that is hard to detect is the "cookie cutter" solution, which occurs when consultants use the same solution(s) for all of their clients or for all clients with similar characteristics. This can save time for consultants. In addition, less reputable consultants become very adept at selling particular solutions, which increases their success ratios at your expense.

The downside to the cookie cutter approach, of course, is that it may not be the best solution for your particular situation. A custom solution would increase the probability that you achieve your financial goals. However, custom recommendations take more time and resources than standard, "canned" proposals.

There is another issue related to this conflict, and you may have unknowingly caused it to happen. When you are reluctant to pay reasonable fees for quality work, the consultant may have no choice but to provide a lower level of service, a modification which is not disclosed to you. In the real world, you get what you are willing to pay for.

For all of these reasons, it is important for you to obtain proposals from multiple consultants. You can compare them to each other and select the one you think best fits your situation. Comparisons also put pressure on consultants to do their best work for you.

Licenses, Certifications, and Associations

Evaluating licenses is one of the easiest ways to determine what type of advisor you are interviewing. Professionals either have the right types of active licenses or they do not. This topic is easy to address, because quality consultants will be more than happy to disclose their licensing to you; misrepresentation that is in writing, however, is a business risk.

Many consultants also hold particular certifications that increase the probability that they have the knowledge you are paying for. A high percentage of them also belong to associations that have continuing education requirements which increase the quality of their advice and provide a venue for interacting with their peers. Licenses, certifications, and association memberships are important credentials and you should know about them before selecting a consultant.

Licenses and Registrations

There are several licenses and one registration that enable professionals to market consulting services and receive fees as the method of compensation:

- The Registered Investment Advisor (RIA) registration is issued by the SEC for consultants who are responsible for more than $25 million, or by the state in which the consultant resides if total assets are less than $25 million.
- Consultants may have their own RIA or be covered by the RIA of the firm for which they work or with which they are licensed.
- Fee-based advisors may hold multiple securities licenses, issued by the NASD, that enable them to receive fee revenues and work in multiple states. The licenses include Series 7, 65, 66, and 63.

Keep in mind that licenses vary by state.

Certifications

The highest-quality certifications for a consultant are those of the Certified Investment Management Analyst (CIMA) and Certified Investment Management Consultant (CIMC). These designations are awarded by the Investment Management Consultant Association (IMCA) after the advisor has completed a course of study and successfully passed a comprehensive test. Ideally, the consultant possesses one or more certifications. The CIMA and CIMC certification merged and there will be no new CIMCs issued after December 31, 2003.

Associations

Consultants who are committed to their profession belong to associations that sponsor continuing education programs and other courses that expand their knowledge base and increase their professionalism. The ideal associations will emphasize both continuing education and integrity. The Investment Management Consultants Association is the premier association in the industry for advisors who provide consulting services.

Minimum Assets

All good consultants set minimum asset requirements with which they are willing to work. In general, the more credentials and experience they possess, the higher the minimums. Consultants have the biggest range of minimums of any type of advisor, so it pays to ask about minimums early in the evaluation process. You do not want to waste their time or yours.

Minimum Fees

A note of caution: a high percentage of consultants publish a minimum fee rather than a minimum asset amount. In this case, you can pay the minimum fee regardless of your asset amount. For example, a consultant has a one percent fee schedule on the first $500,000 of assets (a minimum fee of $5,000). You have $350,000 and want to work with this consultant. You then pay the $5,000 minimum fee regardless of your asset amount. However, if you do, you will pay 1.43 percent ($5,000 divided by $350,000) rather than one percent for the consultant's services. If you want to pay a one percent fee or less, you will have to invest $500,000 or more with the consultant. Your other alternative is to find a consultant with a lower minimum.

Less Than $250,000

Very few consultants will work for percentage fees when you invest less than $250,000 of assets. The reason is simple. They cannot make enough money to justify their time. The reality is that an investor with $90,000 and one with $360,000 take virtually the same amount of time, but the latter generates four times more revenue for the consultant who charges a one percent fee. The smaller the asset amount, the higher the probability that you will pay a minimum fee.

$250,000 to $1,000,000

Most consultants work with investors whose assets are between $250,000 and $1 million because there are more of them. Millions of investors have accumulated these asset amounts and want to invest in the securities markets using the services of money managers. Professionals' most frequent minimums are $250,000, $500,000, and $1 million. These asset amounts will generate enough compensation to justify the consultants' time, although at the lower end of the range, you may experience a reduced level of service. As consultants become more successful, due to the application of increasing competence, their minimum assets or fees are likely to go up.

More Than $1,000,000

Many of the very best consultants in the country have asset minimums of $1 million to $100 million. They work exclusively with high net worth individuals and institutional clients, such as pension plans, endowments, and foundations. They are usually employees of financial services or consulting firms that focus on these marketplaces. Their primary services are the same as consultants with lower minimums; however, most of their work is customized for particular clients. Consultants with lower minimums tend to rely on databases and web-based support services to leverage their time, enabling them to work for investors who own smaller asset amounts with higher levels of efficiency and results.

Types of Assets

There are two main types of consultants: those who work with individuals' assets and those who work with institutional assets. Very few consultants work with both types of assets due to their inherent differences. For example, institutional assets are frequently tax-exempt and overseen by trustees, while a high percentage of individual assets are taxable and controlled by individuals.

Individuals

Individuals have three characteristics that distinguish them from institutions:

1. The asset amounts are usually smaller.
2. The consultant is working with the owner of the assets—you— who has a more intense interest in the results. The entire investment strategy is focused on the needs of one individual or family.
3. A high percentage of your assets are taxable.

Most consultants specialize in working with individuals because there are more potential clients than institutions.

Institutions

Trillions of dollars of assets are owned or controlled by institutions rather than individuals. The pension plans of corporations, public organizations, and Taft-Hartleys (unions) comprise the most common form of institutional assets. Other forms include the foundation and endowment assets of nonprofit institutions, such as hospitals and universities. In all cases, the assets are invested in a tax-exempt environment, which creates unique strategic investment opportunities. Institutions have different rules than individuals, so there are consultants who have developed specialized skills for working with these types of assets. Rarely do consultants have the skills to work with both types of assets, so you want to be sure that you select the right type of professional for your assets.

The Best of the Best

Consultants are the most highly compensated professionals in the financial services industry for a reason—they provide the highest quality advice for a recurring fee revenue stream that goes up with the market. Given the proper knowledge and a choice, every investor would select a consultant as his or her personal financial advisor. If your current advisor is not a consultant, it is most likely that you were not aware of the benefits of working with a consultant, you were not provided a choice, or your asset amount did not justify their services.

Focused Services

Consultants are specialists who are focused on one objective: helping you to achieve your financial goals. They are not planners, tax experts, or attorneys. Their role is to help you invest your assets in a number of classes using the services of multiple money managers who collectively enable you to attain your goals for a minimum amount of risk. Their focus is facilitated by substantial knowledge gained from education and experience. You know exactly what you are paying for when you hire a consultant as your advisor.

The Supply of Consultants

If all investors would be better off with a consultant as their advisor, why are all advisors not consultants? The first answer is the historical compensation system of the industry. For hundreds of thousands of advisors, converting from commissions to fees represents a significant pay cut—a five percent commission to a one percent annual fee. Not only is the commission five times greater, but it is paid upfront; while the fee has to be earned over time. The one percent fee, which is billed quarterly, takes five years to earn the same amount that was paid in commission shortly after the date of the sale. As if this is not enough, the commission-based advisor is paid whether you achieve your goals or not. The fee-based consultant has to earn the revenue or be terminated if you are dissatisfied, in which case the professional's revenue from the relationship stops.

The second reason that more advisors are not consultants is that they lack knowledge. At least 75 percent of all advisors do not have the skills necessary to provide consulting services. They are trained to sell products, not provide high-value, advice-driven services.

Given the pay cut scenario, why are consultants the most highly compensated professionals in the industry? The answer is that they provide services to a critical mass of assets. For example, a consultant with a one percent fee and $100 million of assets generates $1 million of annual revenue. The consultant has one primary objective for clients who own these assets—to make sure that goals are being achieved in order to continue servicing their assets.

Commission to Fee

The transition from commissions to fees is relatively straightforward for the professional. The advisor sends you a letter announcing a change in the business model. The individual is changing from selling to consulting and in the future will only accept fees as compensation for services. The letter should also describe the fee arrangement and may ask you to sign an attached services agreement that describes the new relationship. Assuming the advisor is a qualified consultant, you should welcome a letter of this kind and sign the agreement, because you will receive a much higher level of service.

If you have your assets spread among several commission advisors, you should consolidate them with the professional who has decided to convert to a fee-based consulting practice. Consolidation benefits you once you are working with a consultant.

SUMMARY

- ✔ The ideal type of advisor for your assets is a financial consultant. This professional has the greatest amount of investment knowledge and the fewest conflicts of interest.

- ✔ Consultants are specialists who are positioned between you and the money managers. They help you pick managers, allocate assets, and evaluate performance.

- ✔ Consultants add more value than other types of advisors.

- ✔ Consultants are focused on the achievement of your financial goals.

- ✔ Discretionary consultants add more value than nondiscretionary consultants.

- ✔ You will need at least $100,000 of assets to hire a consultant. Many consultants have even higher asset minimums or they charge minimum fees.

- ✔ Only hire consultants who are fee-based.

8

PLANNERS

More than any other type of professional, financial planners require rigorous due diligence to evaluate their knowledge, integrity, services, conflicts of interest, and methods of compensation. That is because very few planners provide quality services that produce sophisticated plans which increase the probability that you will achieve your financial goals. A much larger percentage of these professionals call themselves planners and use the planning service as a sales strategy for building trust and selling investment products. Because anyone can use the professional title of planner with no disclosure about credentials and because there are more bad planners than good ones, you risk selecting the wrong individual to help you map your financial future.

Planning services began gaining popularity among advisors over twenty-five years ago, when insurance professionals determined that the "agent" designation on their business cards was an impediment to building trust quickly and selling products. There was substantial buyer resistance to insurance products due to the industry's aggressive sales tactics using low-quality agents. However, changing titles from "agent" to "planner" was little more than subterfuge; the real purpose was still to sell copious amounts of insurance products.

Brokers and other sales-oriented financial representatives eventually began marketing planning services for the same reasons that agents were. However, instead of selling life insurance, they sold investment products such as mutual funds and annuities.

Over time, "best in class" planners emerged from these two groups. These professionals began placing more emphasis on the planning process and less emphasis on the sales process. Their role was to produce high-quality plans which you could use to map out your financial future. Today, these exceptional planners are a small subset of the thousands of professionals who call themselves planners. They are also the ones who have a positive impact on the achievement of your goals.

Planning Overview

Planning services are a good idea for millions of investors because plans provide information needed to make financial decisions. For example, planning helps determine how much has to be saved—while allowing for expenditures—in order to achieve long-term financial objectives. Investors who do not have this map are like rudderless ships: they risk running aground and not reaching their destinations.

The primary benefit of a comprehensive planning approach is that the planner looks at all of your financial needs and thus is not limited to the amount of assets that you have available for investment. The other two types of advisors—consultants and financial representatives—are only concerned with issues that directly impact the investment of your assets.

Bad Plans

Financial planning is counterproductive when a professional produces a plan that recommends the purchase of particular products and is more concerned with the sale of those products than the production of a quality plan. Whether or not the plan actually produces the desired result for investors becomes secondary to the sale of financial products.

The ultimate planning risk occurs when you rely on substandard plans to make important financial decisions. You mistakenly believe that this plan is based on quality assumptions, projections, and outcomes. In fact, the inferior plan is nothing more than a technique used by the advisor for gaining access to assets, building trust, and selling financial products. It may take time for you to determine that the plan you purchased for a nominal amount of money is worthless. Now you have to make up for lost time and, as you already know, it is impossible to recover lost years.

The Upside to Planning

A high-quality plan will increase the probability that you will achieve your financial goals. A good plan combines the knowledge of a professional with sophisticated software, enabling you to make critical decisions. These decisions will determine the outcome of your financial future.

It's the Money

It is easy to understand the inherent conflict of interest that exists for planners whose principal objective is the sale of financial products. They sold you planning services but could only make a few hundred or a few thousand dollars in fees for providing the service. However, they can potentially make tens of thousands of dollars when they help you implement the plan. This is a tempting financial opportunity for planners and a true test of integrity. How do they turn down the opportunity to make substantially more money, especially when trust that was developed during the planning process makes it an easy sale? Most planners do not turn it down; it is their primary source of compensation.

Service Combinations

Planners have three possible types of expertise (disciplines) that determine the combination of services they provide during and after the planning process: *planning*, *investments*, and *insurance*. However, many planners deliberately blur the distinctions among these services to capture as many revenue streams as possible from your assets.

Four Service Combinations

There are four possible service combinations that planners can provide: planning only, planning plus investment, planning plus insurance, and planning plus investment plus insurance. Your challenge is to determine if the planners actually have expertise in all the disciplines they say they do. Otherwise, a particular service will be compromised.

Knowledge in Multiple Disciplines

All plans have to be implemented for them to become realities. You have to invest in various financial products to build the asset base necessary to achieve your goals. In addition, you will need life insurance, disability income insurance, and other products that protect you and your family from the unexpected.

The broad scope of the planning process produces several sales opportunities for enterprising professionals. However, this creates a risk for you because the professional may not be proficient in each of the three disciplines. Each one is complex, so it is rare to find planners who are skilled in all three. Notwithstanding the breadth of each expertise area, most planners represent themselves as having interdisciplinary knowledge because they can earn large commissions from the sale of their own product recommendations.

Core Competencies

Planners require several core competencies to produce high-quality plans that will help you achieve your goals. These competencies are derived from various training, certification, and continuing education programs.

Personal Profiles

Planners must know how to obtain comprehensive information necessary to produce a quality plan. Otherwise, you run the risk of a misleading outcome with a low probability of occurrence. This is the financial equivalent of the concept in computing known as GIGO— Garbage In, Garbage Out.

All planning processes are initiated by developing a personal profile that describes your current financial situation, expectations for change, and long-term goals. Planners use future expectations to generate assumptions that will project your current situation into the future. For example, what is your expected income growth rate for the next twenty years until you retire?

A low-end planner will collect the minimum amount of information necessary to complete the planning process using inadequate software. The high-end planner will gather substantial amounts of information, will review complex legal and insurance documents, and will talk to your CPA about tax issues. The more comprehensive the profiling process, the more meaningful the outcome.

Planning Software

All financial plans are produced by software with varying levels of complexity and sophistication. The planner must know how to input data into the system and produce the outcomes for you. The data in your personal profile are the primary inputs used to develop a plan that describes what you should and should not do if you want to achieve your goals. For example, assume that you must save eight percent of your after-tax income for the next 20 years, and you cannot spend more than $87,500 plus inflation on your current cost of living. The software produces a year-by-year summary which you can review and periodically update.

It may also be necessary to modify inputs to produce desired outcomes which still have reasonable probabilities of occurring. Perhaps one of your inputs was too conservative and produced unsatisfactory numbers when projected over long time periods. As an illustration, suppose you estimated a two percent inflation rate but the real rate was closer to three percent. This one percent difference compounded over twenty years will greatly impact the achievement of your goals.

Annual Reviews

Professionals should also be skilled at updating your current plan to reflect changes that occur over time. Numerous types of changes impact your net worth (the performance of the stock market), income (an unexpected promotion and raise), personal situation (a new child), and health (disabling back problems). You and your planner should get together at least once a year to review the most recent data and the underlying assumptions that were used to develop your plan. The purpose of the review is to make sure that the plan is still valid based on your inputs and goals. It should not be confused with quarterly investment performance meetings.

Investment Knowledge

Most professionals who specialize in planning services do not have a substantial amount of investment knowledge because their backgrounds are insurance. They develop a basic plan and invest assets based on the recommendations contained in that plan.

Professionals who work for commissions want to invest your assets because that is how they earn their income. These planners also have limited investment knowledge, because it does not take much to sell mutual funds and annuities. The fact that they can be licensed on Monday and sell financial products the same day tells you that they do not have to know much, especially if they have strong sales skills.

Planners who also have consulting skills have substantial amounts of investment knowledge that they use to develop strategy, allocate assets, select money managers, and report performance. These planners are rare but extremely valuable due to the dual nature of their service.

Risk Management

Planners also have to know how to protect your income and assets from catastrophes such as long-term disability, premature death, and job loss. Your financial plan should include recommendations for insurance policies that minimize these risks or eliminate them altogether. Since many planners are former insurance agents, they are usually knowledgeable about these solutions.

Your financial plan must include a section on risk management. However, you do not have to buy the products from the planner just because the plan calls for a disability income policy. The fact that you need a policy does not necessarily mean that the planner knows the best policy with the lowest price for your situation—this may require the knowledge of a specialist.

Assumptions, Projections, and Probabilities

Good planning is a holistic approach that includes all types of assets, sources of income, expense budgets, and disposition instructions in your will. The most important part of the process involves the assumptions about the future that are used to make projections. All planners should be able to test the probability that the projections will occur and show you the outcomes of various strategies.

Assumptions

One of the reasons why you have to be careful with planning-based investment strategies is that several variables require assumptions to produce the plan. Assumptions create a substantial amount of latitude for planners who make them part of their sales process. For example, some planners will make aggressive assumptions that make you feel good but are completely unrealistic. Conversely, realistic assumptions may have dire consequences that make you feel bad.

Good plans are based on assumptions about the future that can be as conservative or aggressive as you would like them to be. Your savings rate assumption might be 5 percent, 10 percent, or 20 percent of net income. Your rate of return assumption for the stock market might be 8, 10, or 12 percent. Your income assumption could grow wages at an annual rate of 4 or 8 percent until your retirement date. Your inflation assumption could be 2 or 3 percent. Your annual income requirements in twenty years when you retire could be $92,000 or $192,000. All of these long-term projections are based on assumptions.

The more aggressive your assumptions, the less likely it is that they will occur. However, extremely conservative numbers may not be realistic, either. Therein lies the science of planning. It is up to the professional to develop realistic assumptions with you, input them into the planning software system, and then produce projected outcomes. It may be necessary to change the inputs to produce higher-probability plans.

Projections

Once you and your planner have developed data that describe your current situation and assumptions about the future, the planner's software is used to project outcomes for each year of the remainder of your life (usually assumed to be age 90).

The projections answer several critical financial questions:

- Will you have enough assets to achieve all of your goals?
- Will you have adequate income to maintain your desired standard of living for the remainder of your life?
- Will you have enough assets and income to achieve financial security late in life?
- What are the risks that may derail your plans for a comfortable, secure retirement?

Realistic assumptions increase the probability of valid projections, but they have to be tested.

Probabilities

Sometimes planners present projected numbers as if they have a 100 percent probability of occurring. They make the outcomes sound positive to facilitate the sale of financial products. These planners reason that if you do not like the outcomes, you might not buy their products. However, this is not good planning. It is a sales process superimposed on a planning process, and it is very dangerous. It may be years before you know that your plan is flawed.

Outcomes can be very misleading, especially when you are talking about retirement assets and income requirements that are twenty years into the future. This is why simulations which determine the probability that various financial scenarios will occur provide an invaluable service. Extremely conservative assumptions may produce outcomes with a 100 percent probability of occurring; however, they may not meet your long-term needs. Aggressive assumptions may have only a 40 percent probability of occurring. Moderate assumptions may have a 75 percent probability of occurring, and using them might be your most desirable scenario given your current situation and goals.

Compensation Systems

You can determine what type of planner you are evaluating by knowing the individual's method of compensation. A small percentage of professionals charge a fee which reflects their time and billing rates. The vast majority of planners charge commissions when they sell financial products during the implementation phase. In between these two extremes are professionals who do both.

Fee-Only Planners

Fee-only planners work exclusively for fees and will not accept commissions for their services. The fees can be based on fixed or hourly rates. Your preference should be to pay a fixed fee because you will know your out-of-pocket expense in advance. Planners may require hourly fees when it is difficult to estimate the time it will take to produce large, complex plans. They have to charge hourly fees so they receive adequate compensation for their knowledge and time.

Using a fee-only planner is ideal because you know the professional is focused on providing a quality plan that has a high probability of occurring. There is no reason for the individual to manipulate outcomes because there are no financial incentives to do so. Some fee-only planners also have consulting skills that can be used to develop investment solutions that will generate additional fees for the planner.

Commission-Only Planners

The commission-only planner is compensated when you purchase financial products recommended in their plan. Third parties pay planners when they provide services for commissions—usually the third party is the manufacturer of the investment products or the broker/dealer who holds the professional's licenses. There are thousands of product companies, proprietary and third party, that compete for the planner's business—your assets. They pay professionals billions of dollars a year to recommend their products.

Third party payments also create the opportunity for another sales ploy—the "free" financial plan. The product company pays the planner, which makes the service free to you. Right? Wrong. Only inexperienced investors would believe this sales pitch. Investors' payments must cover all of the service providers' expenses or else they go out of business. The suspect planner uses this strategy to compete with reputable planners who charge fees for their services.

For example, assume that the plan recommends purchasing several mutual funds for your IRA. The mutual funds all have back-end loads that pay the advisor a five percent commission. You paid the advisor $10,000 to produce the plan because your assets were valued at $200,000. The result is a very profitable strategy for the planner and a substantial amount of risk for you.

Commission amounts are never made known to you unless you make their disclosure a requirement during the selection process. Advisors may argue that they do not know the amount because the investment solution has not been developed yet. This is an invalid argument. Advisors know how they are going to be compensated before they start the planning process; otherwise, they would not start it. This is why one of their first questions involves your asset amount. Advisors do not want to waste their time or yours if you cannot produce enough income for them.

Fee-and-Commission Planners

This type of planner is out to achieve the best of both worlds with your money. They want to charge fees for the plan (although they are nominal fees) and earn commissions from the sale of financial products during the implementation phase. Many planners use this strategy on gullible investors. The advisors know they can get away with it—especially when they are trusted. A note of caution: planners who accept both types of compensation frequently refer to themselves as fee-based, which is substantially different than fee-only. The fee-based planner is leaving the door open to receive commissions, whereas the fee-only planner has closed that door.

Some planners will also offset fees with commission income. For example, they normally charge a $10,000 fee for their service and receive $5,000 in commissions for the sale of a product. These professionals will reduce the $10,000 fee by the amount of the commission, reducing the cash fee to $5,000. The total fee is still $10,000. This is the ethical way for planners to avoid double dipping when commissions are an unavoidable byproduct of their recommendations—for example, a life insurance policy that pays commissions to the planner.

Asset-Based Planners

A new type of service combination which is based on your asset amount is beginning to take hold. For one all-encompassing fee—say, 1.4 percent, you receive planning and consulting services. This can be an attractive package if the professional has planning and consulting expertise. If not, the next best scenario is to work with a team of professionals, including one who specializes in planning and one who specializes in consulting. The total fee must reflect the value of the professionals' combined services.

Conflicts of Interest

Planners have conflicts of interest due to the unique nature of their relationships with you. It is all about misplaced trust. That is, unscrupulous planners earn your trust in the planning phase of the process and can easily abuse it during the implementation phase. It is up to you to protect your own financial interests. Following is a brief description of the most common conflicts. Conflicts of interest are also described in more detail in Chapter Four.

Disclosure

Rarely do planners offer any form of disclosure about potential conflicts of interest. Instead, it is up to you to ask for the information in writing. Disclosures should include all of the basic information described in Chapter Five: education, experience, certifications, licensing, compensation, conflicts of interest, etc.

Objectivity

You have to question the objectivity of planners who work for commissions and are paid by third parties. Is their principal goal to produce a quality plan for you or to maximize the amount of commissions they earn from your assets? If you believe the latter is the case, as I do, then you run a substantial risk of using recommendations that have little or no long-term value.

Investment Products

When advisors work for commissions, there is always the possibility that their recommendations are not in your best interest. That is, they may recommend low-quality products so they can receive maximum amounts of compensation. These can include proprietary and third party products.

Licensing, Certifications, and Associations

When you select a planner, you want an experienced, knowledgeable professional whose principal goal is to help you develop a roadmap for your financial future. One way that you can increase your odds of selecting the right professional is to review their licenses, certifications, and association memberships. This evaluation will help you select professionals who can produce quality plans and help you avoid those whose principal motivation is the sale of financial products.

Planning Licenses

There are no licensing requirements to be a planner. As such, any professional can call themselves planners. This lack of regulation facilitated the change in job titles of agents and financial representatives to planners. All that these professionals had to do was print new business cards.

Fee-Based Registration

Registration is determined by the planners' method of compensation: fee, commission, or both. Professionals who market their planning and investment services for fees may be Registered Investment Advisors. As with consultants, the SEC or the state in which the advisor resides issues this registration.

Securities Licenses

Planners may hold a Series 6 license that enables them to market financial products for commissions. This is the most obvious indicator that you are dealing with a sales professional who is using a planning service to gain access to your assets.

Planners may also be Series 7 and 65-licensed so they can market securities and financial products for commissions. In some states, these licenses permit advisors to market financial services for fees.

Certifications

Like any other professional, a financial advisor who has committed the time, energy, and money to become certified is a safer bet for you than one who has not. You can assume that you will obtain superior services from a certified professional; they are better educated and have passed a competency test to obtain the certification.

There are four planner designations worth noting. The Certified Financial Planner (CFP) is the most popular type of planner certification. Since 1972, the College for Financial Planning has issued approximately 55,000 CFPs in the United States. Colleges and universities that have developed financial planning curriculums issue the Personal Financial Planner (PFP) designation. The Personal Finance Specialist (PFS) was developed for CPAs who also provide financial services. The Chartered Financial Consultant (ChFC) certification is the fourth and was developed by the insurance industry.

Associations

Planners who are dedicated to their profession and their own personal development also belong to associations. The best associations publish ethical standards and provide numerous learning opportunities for planners. In fact, most have continuing education requirements through which professionals maintain membership. Being part of an association is one of the primary ways that planners can increase their knowledge and learn to develop more sophisticated solutions for you.

There are several noteworthy associations. The one with the highest standards is the National Association of Personal Financial Advisors (*www.napfa.org*), which has 900 members who provide advice. The small number tells you just how few of this type of planners there are. One of the oldest and largest associations (with 29,000 members) is the Financial Planning Association. It has a very solid membership base, and it promotes competence, integrity, relationships, and stewardship. It also offers numerous courses, conferences, and seminars to expand the knowledge of its members. There is also the Institute of Certified Financial Planners, which was formed more than 25 years ago.

Asset Amounts

Asset amounts can impact a planner's willingness to work with you regardless of the method of compensation. For example, one planner might charge a fee of 1.4 percent that includes planning and consulting. As with the consultant, the assets determine the planner's revenue.

Commission planners who market "free" plans can work with smaller asset amounts than their asset-based counterparts because commission rates are high. For example, they can earn $2,500 or more from as little as $50,000 of assets. Compare this to a 1.4 percent fee planner who can only make $700 on the same amount of assets.

Planners who charge flat fees are not concerned about asset amounts, but you might be. Their fee could be $3,500, and it reflects the cost of their time versus your asset amount. If you want a quality plan and have a small amount of assets, you should still consider paying the fee due to the impact that the process has on your financial future.

Under $100,000

Investors with less than $100,000 are most vulnerable to the commission-only or fee-and-commission planner. They have relatively basic needs and are less likely to pay a significant fee for the plan, due to the mistaken belief that all plans are the same. These investors are not the primary target market for the services of fee-only or asset-based planners.

Regardless of your asset amounts, you should pay a fee for planning and not allow planners to participate in the implementation—unless they can prove that they have the necessary knowledge. Even though the fee may seem expensive, it is actually low when compared to the cost of bad advice and its impact on your financial future.

$100,000 to $1 Million

The vast majority of investors who utilize planning services fall into this asset category. Most of the United States' 76 million baby boomers are in this asset range. They are highly sought after by investment professionals because they have a critical mass of assets and most have the potential for significant growth. At the same time, they have sufficient assets to generate reasonable fees or substantial commissions for the planners. The higher the asset amounts, the more the market is dominated by fee-for-service and asset-based planners.

There is an irony here. Let us assume that all investors start off with small amounts of assets and a little bit of knowledge. As their assets grow, so does their knowledge about planners and the services needed to achieve their financial goals. At some point, these investors will not even consider a commission planner.

Over $1 Million

Like consultants, the best planners want to work with individuals who own the largest amounts of assets. The needs of large investors are more complex, and higher fees are more acceptable to them because they have more to lose if the plan does not work.

Many of these planners are current or former tax professionals or attorneys, especially estate and tax specialists. As a group, they have very high skill sets, advanced degrees, certifications, and are members of associations.

The Best in Class

The ideal planner has some very specific characteristics and can provide an optimum plan for your financial future. This planner:

- Provides planning for fixed, hourly, or asset-based fees
- Has a strong background of applicable education and experience
- Utilizes sophisticated planning software.
- Has the ability to simulate outcomes of plans and provide probabilities
- Holds certifications and is a member of various professional associations
- Is willing to provide full disclosure about background, services, compensation, and conflicts of interest
- Is willing to interact with other professionals such as your CPA and attorney

---

SUMMARY

✔ All investors should have a quality plan that is a roadmap for their financial futures.

✔ Planning is an extremely valuable service when delivered by a competent, trustworthy professional for a fee.

✔ A high percentage of all financial planners use the planning process to gain access to your assets.

✔ Too many planners offer cheap or "free" plans and make money from their own recommendations—a major conflict of interest if there ever was one.

✔ Evaluating licensing, certifications, association memberships, and methods of compensation are easy ways to determine the type of planner you are interviewing.

✔ You should use the services of a fee-only planner and not rely on this individual to invest your assets, unless they can pass your due diligence process for investment professionals.

✔ There is no rule that the professional who prepared the plan has to sell you the insurance and investment products recommended in the plan.

9

FINANCIAL REPRESENTATIVES

Financial representatives are the dominant type of advisor who comprise the sales forces of most investment distribution companies. They are part of an old, enduring business model that was based on several axioms that became the foundation for most companies in the industry:

- Financial products are sold and not bought, so companies employ or license hundreds or thousands of representatives to sell their products.
- Investors have limited investment knowledge and are trusting by nature. The two characteristics combined enable the industry to employ inexperienced representatives with limited amounts of knowledge to market its products.
- Representatives with limited skills are less expensive for companies to support, therefore there are more of them.

- It is more expensive to support high value professionals with substantial amounts of expertise, therefore there are fewer of them.

The imbedded belief in these axioms has produced an industry with a sales culture and numerous conflicts of interest, because its goals and those of investors are very different. The bottom line is that the industry achieves its goals for revenue and profit at the expense of investors.

Selling Versus Advising

The two dominant business models in the financial services industry are selling and advising. Make no mistake—they have very little in common. Every company and every advisor has to select one of the two models. Consultants have chosen to be paid for their knowledge and advice. Representatives have chosen to be paid for their sales ability. It is important to note that companies may have both types of advisors. The advisor can choose either model as long as the revenue production of the individual meets the requirements of the company and their own need for income.

Sales Model

Advisors who subscribe to the sales model can be described by five core characteristics:

1. They have much lower levels of investment knowledge than advice-oriented professionals.
2. They are licensed to sell financial products and to be paid with commissions.
3. Their recommendations are based on their need to sell products rather than on helping you achieve your financial goals.
4. They have more conflicts of interest than any other type of advisor.
5. They represent the greatest risk to your financial future.

You have the lowest probability of achieving your goals when it is a representative who is providing investment recommendations.

Advice Model

Advisors who practice the advice model also have five unique characteristics:

1. They have much higher levels of knowledge than sales-oriented professionals. They use this knowledge to develop sophisticated investment solutions for your assets.
2. They are Registered Investment Advisors or are part of an RIA firm, creating a much higher standard for ethics.
3. They work for fees, because they realize you have a need for ongoing services and not just one-time services.
4. They have the fewest conflicts of interest of financial professionals.
5. They are called consultants and they represent the least risk to your financial future.

You always want to be sure that your financial advisor employs the advice model and not the sales model.

Financial Representatives

The financial representative is the one who sells various types of investment products such as mutual funds, annuities, securities, life insurance, and limited partnerships. This individual is paid large commissions for selling these products because they generate high profit margins for the companies that produce them.

Easy to Hire and Train

If you owned a financial services company, you would probably subscribe to the theory that larger numbers of representatives produce more revenue and profit than smaller numbers. In fact, many such companies describe their size in terms of number of advisors—"Our firm has 3,000 licensed representatives." In addition, as the owner of the company, you would believe that a great representative is one who produces the largest amounts of revenue that you can record immediately. Based on these beliefs, you would want to employ or license as many representatives as possible and pay them commissions on the sales they generate.

As you already know, representatives do not require much investment knowledge to sell. All they have to do is pass a relatively easy test, and they can start selling the day they receive their licenses. This reduces the industry's expense for training and development and maximizes revenue and profit.

Ominously, many companies tell new representatives to start the sales process with family members, friends, and associates with whom there is an established relationship and some level of trust. This is a clear message to representatives to take advantage of the people they know in order to gain experience and generate immediate revenue for themselves and their companies. The companies make money, representatives make money, and acquaintances suffer the consequences of questionable recommendations and inexperience.

Types of Financial Representatives

Representatives have used different titles and roles over the years. Most of them change their "old" titles and roles to whatever is most acceptable to you, the investor.

The term agent usually describes sales professionals in the insurance industry, because in the past, their product offerings were limited to various types of insurance products. For example, they sold life, health, disability, and casualty insurance.

Variable annuities and variable universal life are investment products inside insurance contracts. This distinction required insurance agents to obtain securities licenses to market these products. Once agents were licensed, they started marketing mutual funds and other investment products. Today, thousands of them are agents/financial representatives selling insurance and investment products.

Stockbrokers are the other primary type of financial representative. Back when Wall Street was firmly in control of investment information, it was delivered through stockbrokers, who used the information to sell securities to you. Ostensibly, these professionals were helping you build a portfolio of stocks and bonds by recommending particular securities for investment. However, they were compensated for transactions, so the more frequently they could convince you to buy and sell, the more money they made for themselves and their companies.

The traditional role of the stockbroker is going the way of the dinosaur for several reasons. Discount brokers, Internet information companies, mutual funds, and declining commission rates negatively affected brokers' ability to make money. As a result, they needed new ways to generate revenue. A small percentage became consultants, a larger percentage became planners, and the largest percentage became financial representatives. Instead of selling securities, they now use their sales skills to sell financial products.

It is important to note that financial representatives can use any title they choose without breaking any industry rules. Therefore, representatives may call themselves financial consultants, advisors, planners, or any other title that facilitates the sale of financial products. The only way you can protect yourself is to understand the characteristics of quality professionals and use a due diligence process that eliminates the pretenders.

The Impact of a Sales Culture

Sales cultures spawn practices that are used to convince you to buy Wall Street's products. Most financial representatives use similar ones in order to win your assets. It is important for you to understand these techniques so that you can recognize them when they are used to influence your investment decisions or gain control of your assets.

Sales Versus Knowledge

Put yourself in the role of a branch manager who is responsible for 20 financial representatives. Your bonus and future at the company are based on the amount of revenue that your advisors generate each month. In this environment, would you be exhorting your representatives to attend more classes to expand their knowledge or to spend more time selling products? It is always the latter. In fact, for some companies, training and development are viewed as counterproductive and little or no money is budgeted for them. These activities increase expenses and reduce short-term revenue.

Relationships

There is an old adage in the financial services industry which says that "money moves on trust." For the representative, step one in winning your assets is to develop trust as quickly as possible. The representative may do this through friendly referrals, entertainment, establishing common interests, or spending time with you to build rapport. Regardless of the technique that is used, the goal of the representative is to build a relationship that facilitates the sale of financial products. After decades of research, the industry knows that you will not buy if you are distrustful. As a result, representatives have adapted their sales techniques: they start by building trust, then move to selling higher-margin products once trust is established. This relationship-building process enables many representatives to brag that their clients trust them so much, they can sell them anything.

Information Gathering

Consultants gather information in order to develop high-quality solutions that best meet your needs. Financial representatives gather information in order to know what to sell. Are you a candidate for an equity product or a bond product? Should they sell you an annuity or a mutual fund? Remember most representatives do not have the knowledge to develop sophisticated solutions, so they gather information as part of their sales process. Just because they ask questions does not mean that they are interested in helping you achieve your financial goals.

Advice and Sales

The most important question is whether or not representatives are giving dependable advice when they recommend the purchase of investment products. The answer is *no* and *yes*. It is no when advisors know what they want to sell before they meet you. For example, a representative works for Acme Financial and recommends three of the Acme mutual funds to you. It is likely that the intent of the representative was to sell Acme Funds, regardless of your needs, your goals, or the quality of the funds before even walking through the door.

However, if the representative presented you with six funds from three different mutual fund families and helped you choose the best one for your situation, then some advice was part of the sale. However, even this advice is subject to manipulation. The representative's company may have had agreements with particular product companies for undisclosed revenue sharing. In this case, it may have been the real motivation for recommending particular products.

The point is that some financial representatives provide advice, but it is limited by their lack of knowledge, their licenses, and their companies. If they provided more value, they would be high-end planners or consultants. The challenge for you is to determine the quality and intent of their recommendations. All you can do is put them through an intensive due diligence process prior to accepting the advisors' recommendations.

Sales Model and Value

Financial representatives are not paid to add value, because doing so takes knowledge and time—time that could be spent selling even more products. The more investors that representatives talk to, the more sales they generate and the more commissions they earn. Value is added when advisors possess enough knowledge and integrity to provide high-quality, objective advice that helps you achieve your goals.

Who Wins?

There are three winners when you buy financial products from a sales professional: the representative, the representative's company, and the financial product company, which could also be the representative's employer. Representatives earn commissions and companies achieve their goals for revenue and profit. If you are lucky, the products you purchased may provide reasonable returns. However, your luck is not related to the income of the sales professionals and companies. They are paid whether you receive reasonable returns or not.

Service After the Sale

Any advisor who is paid a one-time revenue stream, such as a commission, does not have any economic incentive to service what has been sold. The strategy is to move on to the next sale that generates a new commission. Most industry experts will tell you that service in a commission-based relationship is a myth, because it is a formula for going out of business. There is no revenue stream, unless the advisor works for the manufacturer of the product, to offset the additional expense of providing ongoing service.

Limited After-Sale Services

You should not expect after-sale service, because the representative is not paid by the product companies to provide ongoing service. Once a representative has your assets, the job is done—you will only see the advisor the next time there is a sales opportunity. Examples of after-sale services include monitoring of investments, performance reports, strategic reviews, replacement of underperforming managers, and personal meetings. These are essential services, and they are only provided when the professional is compensated with an ongoing fee.

Trailing Commissions

A form of commission is referred to as a trailer, or ongoing commission. Because some representatives prefer to annuitize revenue streams, making them continuous, some product companies pay smaller commissions upfront and then trailing commissions for the life of the relationship. This is a smart strategy for companies, because upfront expenses are reduced and advisors are compensated with ongoing revenue streams which they hope will improve their investor retention rates. In addition, more contact with investors could mean additional sales in the future.

The fact that a representative is paid a trailer does not mean that you will receive the same level of service as you would from a fee-based consultant. It costs money to provide consulting services; one-time revenue streams and small trailers do not produce sufficient revenues to provide quarterly performance reports and other expense-generating services.

A trailer is still a type of commission because the representative does not have to provide service to earn it. The professional earns it when you invest in the product. In addition, this cost is passed on to you in the form of higher fees from the product provider.

Licensing, Certifications, and Associations

As stated earlier, one of the easiest ways to identify the type of advisor you are evaluating is to review the individual's licensing. Fee advisors and commission representatives have different licenses. In addition, representatives have fewer certifications and association memberships, because they rely on individual sales skills rather than investment knowledge to make a living.

Licensing

By definition, all financial representatives have securities licenses (most often, the Series 6) that permit the sale of financial products for commissions. Any professional who only holds a Series 6 license represents potential risk to you and your financial future.

Representatives can also have other securities licenses such as the Series 7 and 63, which does not mean they are fee-based consultants. They can hold these licenses and still choose to sell financial products to make a living. This decision is usually a function of a limited skill set and the desire for commission rates that are higher than fees.

The ideal licensing for advisors is the Registered Investment Advisor issued by the SEC and individual states. However, it would be rare for financial representatives to have this type of registration. They have no need for one.

Certifications

Financial representatives may hold certain types of certifications, which are usually earned to expand the advisors' product knowledge. For example, some representatives are certified as Mutual Fund Specialists (MFS). The Chartered Life Underwriter (CLU) is a certification that is issued by the insurance industry. Both designations indicate higher levels of product knowledge for the representatives who have them.

Associations

Numerous associations enroll the hundreds of thousands of financial representatives as members. Like their fee-based counterparts, representatives who belong to associations exhibit a greater commitment to their profession than those who do not.

Investment Knowledge

Financial representatives have the least amount of investment knowledge of the three types of advisors. They do not have to know much to sell financial products. A good analogy is the car salesperson, who does not have to know how the engine is built to sell the car. A limited need for knowledge is the primary reason why representatives frequently hold entry-level positions in the industry. As they gain knowledge from experience and education, they modify their business models to provide additional services and work with larger asset amounts.

Level of Knowledge

Most firms that employ or license the services of representatives provide them with little or no training. In some cases, the training budget is less than $100 per advisor per year. In other cases, there is no training budget except to meet the requirements of the regulators.

There is also the issue of "knowing just enough to be dangerous." This saying could have been written specifically for the financial services industry. Most financial representatives know more than the typical investor about mutual funds and insurance products, which makes them the perceived "experts." Because investors see representatives as experts, they listen to their recommendations. This perception contributes to the dysfunctional relationship between investors and many investment professionals.

Conflicts of Interest

As you might imagine, a relationship with a financial representative can be riddled with conflicts of interest. It starts with their representing themselves as experts, continues through the sales process that they use to win your trust, and concludes with the mediocre results they frequently produce for your assets. Every conflict of interest you can imagine is seen with this type of advisor. Most representatives put their interests and those of their companies well ahead of yours.

Hope You Do Not Ask

When financial representatives use a sales process to win your assets, their carefully crafted presentations are designed with one purpose in mind—to convince you to turn your assets over to them. During their presentations, many representatives hope you do not ask key questions which will force them to disclose their weaknesses. However, these questions are extremely important to you. You need to be able to make an informed decision on whether to hire the representative or not. All you have to learn is to ask key questions to offset their sales techniques. This is a short version of the more comprehensive due diligence process that is recommended in Chapter Six. Examples of questions that you should ask are as follows:

- How are they compensated, who compensates them, and in what amounts?
- How long have they been financial representatives?
- What licenses do they hold?
- Are they marketing any proprietary products or products that share revenue with them or their companies?
- Do they provide any services after the sale such as performance reports, monitoring services, and quarterly review meetings?

The answers to these questions will tell you what type of an advisor you are interviewing.

Quality Representatives

The fact that a financial representative is a sales professional represents a conflict of interest because the individual could have chosen to be a competent, trustworthy consultant or planner, putting your interests at the top of the list. Granted, this takes a higher skill set and additional licensing, but it is a small price to pay to be a real advisor.

Having said that, some financial representatives are of a higher caliber and have fewer conflicts of interest than others. This may be the result of the policies of the companies they work for or their own personal integrity. Regardless of the reason, you should still use the due diligence process described in this book to determine their quality and identify their weaknesses.

Asset Amounts

If you have smaller amounts of assets, there is a high probability that you will end up working with a financial representative. You may have limited choices when an appropriate evaluation process is in place; you will have to be exceptionally cautious when you select a representative as your advisor.

Why Use Their Services?

You might be asking yourself: *Why use the services of representatives when they represent so much risk?* The answer is that the nominal amount of knowledge representatives do have may produce a better solution for your assets than what you could achieve on your own. In other words, some help is often better than no help. You just have to be very sure that the representative satisfies your due diligence process before you turn any assets over to the individual. Pay particular attention to the professional's disclosures.

Under $100,000

If you have less than $100,000 of assets available for investment, you are the most vulnerable to the solicitations of financial representatives. It is very important for you to complete a thorough due diligence process to select the best representative you can find; otherwise, you will have to do the investment work yourself.

$100,000 to $500,000

You are in the "gray zone" if you have this asset amount. You have enough assets to hire a fee-based professional, but may not have enough to obtain the services of high-end consultants. Given a choice, you should never hire a commission advisor when you have the opportunity to hire one who is fee-based.

Over $500,000

Very few investors with more than $500,000 use the services of a financial representative. Why? First, they have enough assets to obtain the services of high-quality, fee-based professionals. Second, they have no doubt gone through a learning curve while accumulating that asset amount. Third, there is a high probability that they have had bad experiences with lower-quality representatives along the way. As a result, most investors with these asset amounts do not even consider representatives who work for commission.

Proprietary Products

Financial service companies that manufacture their own products (referred to as proprietary products) frequently employ their own professionals to sell these products. If this occurs, they may limit what the representatives sell to proprietary products. This strategy has become more difficult to execute because investors have become more knowledgeable about choices. In response, companies modified this strategy. Now, these firms only try to control a percentage of your assets—say, 50 percent—with their proprietary products.

Where Are the Benefits?

There is no question that most financial services companies are capable of producing some quality products. However, no company produces superior products 100 percent of the time. For example, a typical company with 100 mutual funds might have this result: 10 are excellent, 20 are good, 40 are mediocre, and 30 are terrible. The reason that you want choices from an objective source is so you can choose from the ten excellent funds. You then want to be able to choose excellent funds from other fund groups. There are no net benefits to you when a representative limits your choices to any particular group or groups of products. You are always better off with unlimited choices. You want to select the best funds from all of the fund families.

Who Are the Winners?

Representatives and companies win when they convince you to buy proprietary products. Although the regulators frown on the practice, representatives can earn higher commissions and bonuses for the sale of these products. The companies are the biggest winners of all because their own products carry much higher profit margins than third party products—hence the higher compensation for representatives.

Compensation

One of the easiest ways to identify financial representatives is by their method of compensation. They are always commission-based which includes front, back, level, and trailing commissions. In most cases, they are not even licensed to receive fees for their services.

Commissions

Commission-based transactions create conflicts. An example of how commissions work is the best way to describe the multiple conflicts. Assume that an advisor sells you five mutual funds from a well-known family of funds for your $100,000 of assets. Compensation for the sale is a $5,000 commission. The representative receives 50 to 90 percent of that amount, with the balance going to the employer or licensing company.

Immediate Payouts

Most forms of commission are paid when the sale occurs because the product companies know that instant gratification is the best way to motivate sales-oriented representatives. Deferred compensation reduces motivation. Some product companies even pay weekly to maximize the motivation of the representatives.

Quality Makes a Difference

Lower-quality products frequently pay higher commissions than higher-quality products. This is particularly true in the case of insurance products. Whenever you see excessive compensation go to a representative, it is a red flag. There is a very high probability that the representative and the company behind the professional are not trustworthy. The representative chose to sell inferior products for higher compensation.

The Old Pro

Every product-oriented company has several old pros who have been in the business for years, have large numbers of clients, and produce substantial amounts of commissions. They have built a trusting clientele over the years and have taken good enough care of them to keep them. This does not contradict the sales model description earlier in this chapter. It simply means that there are a few professionals who have built substantial, enduring businesses selling products for commissions. Their base is made up of several hundred or several thousand clients, so they always have new sales opportunities.

SUMMARY

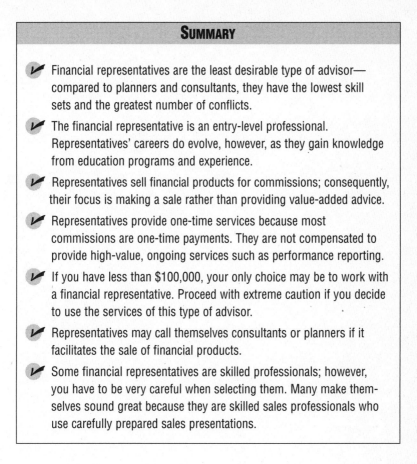

✔ Financial representatives are the least desirable type of advisor—compared to planners and consultants, they have the lowest skill sets and the greatest number of conflicts.

✔ The financial representative is an entry-level professional. Representatives' careers do evolve, however, as they gain knowledge from education programs and experience.

✔ Representatives sell financial products for commissions; consequently, their focus is making a sale rather than providing value-added advice.

✔ Representatives provide one-time services because most commissions are one-time payments. They are not compensated to provide high-value, ongoing services such as performance reporting.

✔ If you have less than $100,000, your only choice may be to work with a financial representative. Proceed with extreme caution if you decide to use the services of this type of advisor.

✔ Representatives may call themselves consultants or planners if it facilitates the sale of financial products.

✔ Some financial representatives are skilled professionals; however, you have to be very careful when selecting them. Many make themselves sound great because they are skilled sales professionals who use carefully prepared sales presentations.

10

REPLACEMENT

If you already have an advisor, you should apply the due diligence process described in Chapter Six to avoid surprises that will compromise your financial future. You most likely did not hire your advisor with the objective process described in this book, so there may be several advisor-related issues that could impact the achievement of your goals. It pays to be cautious when your financial future is at stake.

If you decide to replace your current advisor, there is a structured process you should follow that will minimize your investment risk and out-of-pocket expense in making the change. You will be terminating a relationship with the advisor who recommended particular allocations and money managers. The reason that you are changing is because you are dissatisfied with the current professional's advice. Therefore, it is reasonable to assume that the new advisor will recommend substantial changes to your strategy, allocations, and managers.

Realistic Advisor Expectations

Evaluating a current advisor should start with a review of your expectations in regard to the quality of the individual's services. You will never maintain a long-term advisor relationship if your expectations are unrealistic. There are always reasons to terminate a relationship. The question is whether your reasons warrant termination or some other type of response.

You do not want to fall into the trap of replacing advisors every few years. This only reduces your performance and increases your expenses. Your real goal should be to make sure that you have a quality professional (which may require you to terminate an existing relationship) and then stay with that professional for years.

Market Conditions

Advisors are not magicians. They cannot produce substantial gains in down markets. In fact, they may not even beat particular market indices if they have diversified your assets into multiple classes. For example, suppose that your expectation was to outperform the S&P 500 in rising markets when stocks outperformed bonds. However, your advisor recommended a portfolio that consisted of a blend of stocks and bonds. The result is that your portfolio would not have beaten the S&P 500 in positive years due to the bond component. However, you should have beaten it handily during down years when bonds outperformed stocks. If the stock portion of your investments is similar to the S&P 500, then that portion of your assets should have beaten the index.

Relative Performance

Your performance expectations should always be based on relative standards and never on absolute standards. For example, you may require an advisor to achieve 12 percent absolute returns per year or you will fire the individual. First, this requires a very high tolerance for risk, which you may not have. Second, every advisor in America would be terminated in down or flat markets—a fixed return in fluctuating markets simply does not work.

You will never have a successful long-term relationship with advisors if they are held to absolute standards. Using a relative standard means that the advisor has to beat something, such as inflation, a risk-free return, or a specific market index like the S&P 500. A frequent requirement is to beat a combination of weighted market indices, thereby creating a benchmark. For example, if 60 percent of your assets are invested in the stock market and 40 percent in the bond market, your benchmark would be a blended return of the appropriate equity (stock) and fixed income (bond) indices. The benchmarks should match, as closely as possible, the characteristics of your portfolios. For example, you should not compare the performance of a large-capitalization manager to a small-capitalization index, which would be the equivalent of comparing apples to oranges. Portfolio results versus benchmarks are the primary way to identify performance problems.

Net Returns

Your expectations should be based on *net returns* that are produced for your assets, not on gross returns. With net returns, you have to deduct all fees and commissions from the returns and then compare the results to benchmarks. Advisors are prone to show you gross returns for two reasons: the higher returns make them look better, and net returns are more difficult to calculate. Taxes also reduce your net returns; therefore, an advisor's strategy that produces significant taxable events is not producing the same net returns as a strategy with lower taxable events.

Risk-Adjusted Returns

You should also evaluate advisors based on the amount of risk to which they expose your assets. If you are an aggressive investor, and have exposed your assets to substantial volatility, then you should expect high returns in good years and significant negative returns in bad years.

However if you are a conservative investor and have exposed your assets to minimal risk, then you should expect lower relative returns in up years and smaller negative to somewhat positive returns in down years. High risk and low returns do not go together, just as low risk and high returns do not. Remember, there is no free lunch when you invest in the securities markets.

The Time Period

Give advisors a reasonable amount of time to produce the results you are seeking before taking any action to terminate them. Consultants usually give money managers fixed or variable time periods to perform. A fixed time period is three years. A variable time period is a full market cycle, which is a combination of an up and a down market.

Recent market conditions should also be considered when evaluating an advisor. For example, if you hire an advisor at the beginning of a down market and one year later you have experienced a negative return, it should not be a big surprise. It is also not a reason to terminate the advisor. A major cause for concern would be if you lost significantly more than the market's negative rate of return. Even then, you may have a distorted view of your advisor's ability, because you may have taken more risk than the market. In this situation, the advisor deserves more time than the one year in which you experienced negative returns.

You may have your own timeline based on the amount of confidence that you have in your advisor. When this confidence erodes below a certain point, you will be prone to terminate the advisor. This could take one, two, or three years, but it should never be after just one or two bad quarters. In addition, the erosion of confidence should never be the only reason that you terminate an advisor relationship. Your decision should be more objective than that.

Service Levels

You should also have realistic expectations about the service level you receive from your advisor. Remember, this service level is based on your amount of assets. If you have an excellent advisor but a relatively small amount of assets, you cannot expect the advisor to spend a lot of time with you. For example, if you have less than $500,000, you should expect in-person meetings two times a year. If you have more than this amount, quality advisors are willing to meet with you quarterly and upon request; however, the higher level of service may depend on your proximity to the advisor.

In quarters when there are no in-person meetings, you should expect a phone call or emails with commentary on your results for the most recent period and year to date. Advisors should also be accessible to you by telephone and email with response times of less than 24 hours. If your expectations for personal service are not being met, you should discuss the issue with your advisor. It may not be a reason to terminate the professional if the individual can provide a level of service with which both parties are comfortable.

Reasons for Replacing Advisors

When you hire advisors for the wrong reasons, you are prone to terminate them for the wrong reasons. For example, if you hired the advisor with the expectation of superior results during all market conditions, then you terminated the professional when your expectations were not met—you hired *and* fired for the wrong reasons. Performance, personal service, and fees directly impact your financial well-being and are easy to identify and measure. More subtle issues also impact the quality of your relationships with advisors.

Advisor Ethics

Poor ethics is the number one reason to terminate your relationship with an advisor. How can you possibly turn over your financial future to an advisor who is not completely trustworthy? If an advisor lies to win your assets and you find out about it later, you can never trust this advisor again. Liars will break any commitments they have made—after all, they broke a commitment to tell the truth in the selection process.

You should be able to detect a lack of integrity whenever advisors fail to disclose important information that impacts your selection or retention decisions. Misrepresentation and omissions are also grounds for the immediate termination of the relationship with your advisor. In these cases, the advisor is not providing you with all the information that you require.

The real challenge is not terminating the advisor. Rather, it is determining if the advisor deserves to be terminated. You have to be knowledgeable enough to identify any lack of disclosure, misrepresentation, omission, and conflict of interest. When you do, the advisor should be terminated immediately. You should give the individual no opportunity to make good on broken promises. Talk is usually a sales process that is designed to protect an advisor's economic interests and not yours.

Level of Competence

At some point, you may determine that your advisor lacks the competence to help you achieve your goals. In order to determine this, you have to know enough to identify any deficiencies. Misrepresenting competence in the selection process is grounds for immediate termination—in this case, the issue is trust and not knowledge.

Incompetence manifests itself in the quality of advice you receive. For example, incompetent recommendations could lead to your assets being allocated improperly. Another frequent problem is underperforming managers being recommended because the advisor could not recognize competence in personnel.

There are numerous ways that you may identify incompetence. Once you are aware that your advisor is not competent to handle your assets, you have to change advisors. Otherwise, there is no way that you will achieve your financial goals.

Lack of Performance

Your advisor will recommend several money managers to invest your assets in the securities markets. You can then evaluate the performance of the managers compared to various indices that are similar to the managers' style of management. The collective results of all the managers are indicative of the performance of the advisor. You relied on the advisor's research and advice when you selected the managers.

Even though lack of integrity should be the number one reason to terminate an advisor, underperformance is the more frequent reason because it is easier to identify. For example, based on an average market return of 12 percent for the past three years, you expected a 12 percent return on your assets because you took the same risk as the market. However, your actual return was six percent, lagging the market by six percent per year. You decide to terminate the advisor for insufficient performance.

Ironically, your expectations may have been based on the representations of the advisors during your selection process—especially if you relied on sales presentations to make your decisions. Many advisors sell performance to win your assets without mentioning the low probabilities that it will actually be achieved. The result is that you have unrealistic expectations and will eventually terminate the advisor.

Excessive Expenses

Excessive expenses are another reason to terminate your relationship with an advisor. Again, the challenge is to identify the excess, which could be in the form of commissions, various types of fees, or transaction expenses. If you do not require advisors to disclose their compensation, you will never know if their compensation was too high relative to the time and value they added to the investment process. This is why disclosure is a critical component of your due diligence process.

Quality of Service

Investors also change advisors because their level of service did not meet expectations in five areas:

1. Performance reports were received late; the information thus had little or no value.
2. Reports contained numerous errors and were difficult to read.
3. Advisors were not accessible in a timely manner.
4. Advisors were not prepared to answer questions and provide value-added input at review meetings.
5. Advisors did not provide a proactive level of service.

Conflicts of Interest

Investors frequently identify conflicts of interest after they hire advisors, because their investment knowledge and awareness increases over time. You may become aware that an advisor sold you proprietary products with inferior track records and excessive expenses after the fact. Or an advisor might recommend frequent manager changes because the process generates additional personal income. Once you identify conflicts of interest, you have to replace the advisor, for no other reason than the possibility that other conflicts which you failed to identify might exist. At a minimum, you know that the advisor will fail to put your interests first.

The Replacement Process

Although most of this book is devoted to describing how you select new advisors, this chapter is devoted to the process of terminating current advisors. This triggers the need to find new ones. Replacing an advisor should not be taken lightly, because you do not want to go through the process every few years. If you replace advisors often enough, you will eventually run out of the time you need to compound returns, seriously jeopardizing the achievement of your financial goals.

Identify and Document Concerns

Step one is to identify and document all of your concerns in writing. These concerns can include performance, service, timeliness of reports, expenses, levels of risk, volatility, turnover, or any other issues that concern you. It is very important that you develop the list of concerns without assistance from the advisor, who might otherwise try to counter your concerns with sales skills.

The Warning Letter

You have to make a choice for the next step. Are you willing to give the advisor time to correct a problem, or is your intent immediate termination? For example, if the problem is performance, you may want to give the professional more time. If the problem is competence or integrity, then reasonable amounts of time will not fix it.

If you are going to give the advisor more time, then the next step is a warning letter detailing your concerns. Never communicate your concerns verbally, because you want your concerns to be properly documented in writing for any future discussions or negotiations. In addition, written complaints carry more weight than verbal ones in the financial services industry.

Your letter is a warning which unequivocally states that unless your concerns are addressed quickly, the relationship will be terminated. It also describes the type of response that you are seeking from the advisors. The response must:

- Be in writing
- Provide a description of the real reason for the problem(s)—not sales fluff
- Include a description of the advisor's strategy for addressing your concerns

- Describe a timeline for the implementation of a revised strategy
- Provide a deadline for measuring the efficacy of the strategy

The Termination Letter

If the problems are severe enough or you are simply dissatisfied with the advisor's responses, then the next step is to write a termination letter. It should describe the reasons for the termination with instructions that cover the following topics:

- What the advisor can and cannot do with the assets until they are moved. For example, you might state that the individual is not allowed to initiate any changes in allocations or managers. This will be the responsibility of the new advisor. In addition, you do not want any last-minute activity that produces additional income for the terminated advisor.
- The name of the new custodian. The new advisor will have you complete the forms to move assets to the new custodian.
- The timing of the move to the new custodian.
- A request for a refund of any unearned fees that were paid in advance.
- A final performance report through the last day of your former advisor's responsibility for your assets.

Transition Expenses

If you pay your advisor a fee and there are no commissions of any kind, you may incur minor processing fees for moving your assets to a new custodian. However, if you pay commissions for transactions on separately managed accounts, be aware that there can be significant transaction costs to liquidate one manager's portfolio and buy the new manager's portfolio.

Unearned Fees

Do not forget that most advisors and managers bill quarterly in advance. If you terminate the managers along with the advisors, then both may owe you a refund of their unearned fees. The amount that they owe is calculated after the expiration of the notice period. The issue of a refund should be documented in your termination letter.

Penalty Fees

You should be aware of possible financial penalties when you terminate relationships with advisors who sold you commission products. Sometimes the penalties are called Contingent Deferred Sales Charges and can be effective for seven to fifteen years. For example, the financial penalty might be seven percent of your assets in year one, six percent in year two, five percent in year three, and so on. This is the way that financial product companies protect themselves for commissions paid to the advisors at the time of the sale. If you sell the product during the first few years, the companies recapture the upfront commissions from your assets with the penalty. Your termination letter should cover this issue if you own commission products that include mutual funds, annuities, and life insurance with penalties for early terminations. You do not want any surprises.

Transition

Think of transition as the movement of your assets. When you change advisors, there is usually a change in custodians and sometimes money managers. You have two options: liquidate your current portfolio and transfer cash to the new custodian, or transfer your current holdings intact and let the new advisor and managers make the liquidation decisions.

You were dissatisfied with performance, so it is likely that you were invested with underperforming managers. Therefore, the new advisor will almost certainly want to make changes, which means that one or all managers will be fired and the securities in their portfolios will be sold. If you have already hired the replacement advisor, the new professional can provide you with the transition instructions to send to the current advisor. The instructions are always sent with the termination letter.

Out of the Market

You will not be invested for a period of time when you sell your securities or mutual funds and transfer the proceeds to the new custodian. This time period starts when your current investments are sold and ends when the new investments are purchased—a matter of days or weeks. There may be additional out-of-market time before the new managers invest the proceeds of the sales. After the transfer process is complete, some managers prefer to "phase" new clients into the market—usually 90 days.

The equity markets move in short spurts—think of 300-point days and 1000-point weeks that can occur at any time. The spurts can be upward or downward; however, history shows that markets go up more than they go down. As a result, there is a bigger chance of losing than winning when you are out of the market.

You can avoid this risk by transferring securities to the new advisor. You will stay invested, even though there may be no active management for a period of time. You should make this an important strategic issue with your new advisor.

The Replacement Advisor

Ideally, you will have hired the replacement advisor before you terminate the current advisor. This makes the transition process much simpler since you will have already completed the documents for hiring the advisor, selecting the managers, opening accounts with the new custodian, and transferring assets. You want the new advisor to be accountable for a smooth, painless transition. This is the professional's first opportunity to win your trust and loyalty by providing an efficient process that minimizes lost performance, risk, expenses, and taxes.

Responsibilities

The terminated advisor continues to be responsible for the assets until they have officially left that advisor's control, which happens when the assets leave the original advisor's custodian and you have taken away the responsibility in your termination letter. The new advisor is responsible for monitoring the transfer process until it is completed.

Taxes and Expenses

The transition from one custodian to another can create taxable events, which is one reason why replacing advisors should not be taken lightly. The value of your assets will likely decline in the short-term, but it is a necessary consequence if you want to improve future results. If your accounts are taxable (such as with joint, personal, or trust accounts) and you have gains in your investments, then there will be capital gains taxes if they are liquidated. It is the responsibility of the new advisor to minimize the tax consequences for you during the transition to new managers.

Advisor Responses

Virtually all advisors will object to being terminated for obvious reasons—they will lose out on future fees and commissions from your assets. In addition, sales-oriented professionals know that it is easier to salvage a current relationship than to win a new one. In addition, a professional knows that you may tell your acquaintances that you had a bad experience with that advisor. Negative publicity, especially in smaller cities, can damage advisors' reputations and future earnings potential. Advisors utilize numerous tactics for delaying or avoiding termination.

Buying Time

Professionals who are to be terminated will always try to buy time. They might ask for another quarter, six months, or year to straighten out the problem. Depending on the problem, this strategy works to their benefit, not yours. There are several issues when they buy time:

- They rarely have a carefully planned strategy. They are hoping that time will solve the problem.
- Rarely can serious problems be resolved in months. Poor performance, for example, requires significant time to improve.
- They continue to earn fees and commissions during this period.

If you followed the termination process described in this book, you have already given the advisor time to take corrective action between warning and termination letters. If you succumb to sales pressure, make the waiver of all advisor fees and commissions a condition of the time extension.

Deflecting the Blame

If the core problem is performance, some advisors will try to place all of the blame on the securities markets. There is some validity to this argument, which is why you want relative standards for measuring the performance of advisors and managers. There is no question that advisors produce negative returns during down years. The issue is the *magnitude* of the problem. If the market is down ten percent and you are down 20 percent with the same level of risk, then only half the decline can be explained by market movement, not all of it. In addition, if you were told that your investments were less risky than the market, then you should have been down less than ten percent, and thus have a reason for termination.

Advisors might also try to blame your investment policy, claiming that your allocations, risk tolerances, or restrictions are the source of the problem. This is a weak argument, because the advisors had ample opportunity for input when you were originally developing the policy. In fact, your policy was probably based on their prototypes and recommendations with few or no changes made by you.

Some advisors may actually try to blame you for the problems on the basis that you are the ultimate decision maker. This is also a poor argument; you were relying on their advice to make decisions.

Selective Memory

Less scrupulous advisors use selective memory to their advantage. That is, they are selective about what they remember. They recall conversations that benefit them while disavowing any knowledge of discussions that are adverse to their interests, particularly if those discussions occurred over a period of years. This is the key reason why you must document instructions and other important communications in writing. You never want to have disputes come down to your word against their selective recall.

Dragging Their Feet

As you might imagine, advisors are in no hurry to complete the documents that will transfer assets away from them and on to a new advisor and custodian. The longer they retain the assets, the longer they can earn fees and commissions.

Your best way to encourage timely action is to always communicate in writing and use a messenger service to deliver your instructions and confirm receipt. Failure to follow your directions could cause regulatory problems for the advisor and the advisor's firm. You have to be particularly careful if you know that your advisor lacks integrity. The advisor who abuses trust during the relationship, will likely abuse it after you have terminated services as well.

Fee-Based Versus Commission-Based Advisors

Most fee-based advisors have a 30-day notice period until their expenses stop. Once the notice period expires, so do their expenses.

Commission-based advisors are paid for transactions or sales. Consequently, when they offer to liquidate portfolios for you, it may be a way for them to generate additional commissions for themselves. It is a much better strategy for you to terminate this type of advisor, move the assets to the fee-based advisor, and let this individual liquidate current investments. In a fee-only environment, there are no commissions.

Expect Substantial Changes

You should expect substantial changes when new advisors take over. They will review your current strategies and make recommendations that are intended to improve results. They will develop a new investment strategy and policy. They will change your allocations to various asset classes and replace all or most of your old managers with higher-performing or lower-risk alternatives.

Retain Good Managers

It stands to reason that not everything the previous advisor did was wrong or of low enough quality to justify immediate replacement by your new advisor. Some investments or managers should be retained for the following reasons:

- They were providing competitive returns for your assets.
- Replacement might create a taxable event.
- Replacement will increase your expense structure.
- Replacement will trigger the payment of a financial penalty.
- The new advisor happens to also recommend the manager whom you are considering retaining.

Liquidity

Fee-based advisors usually recommend liquid investments for your assets, although there are exceptions such as hedge funds. Certain types of commission products have contracts that protect the product companies through the use of penalties. These contracts are designed to reduce liquidity by making it expensive to move assets. Be aware of your contractual obligations before moving assets.

A New Custodian

There are three types of custodians: advisor/company, third parties, and product providers. The company that employs or licenses the advisor may be the custodian. Third parties are primarily broker/dealers and banks, while product providers are typically mutual fund and annuity companies. The product providers may use the services of a third party if they do not provide these services internally.

Consultants

You may hire a consultant to replace another consultant or financial representative. Rarely would a consultant replace a planner who only provides planning because these two professionals deliver different services. It is a different issue if the planner also provides financial advice. In this case, you may want to retain the planning service but replace the financial advice component, especially if this individual is acting in the capacity of a financial representative.

Replacing fee-based advisors is easy. Replacing commission-based advisors is more complex because the product company's interests are more impacted. The best example of the additional complexity is the termination charge.

Planners

You can expect the new planner to review and modify all of your existing plans. The professional will charge you a fee for this service, which may replace a superficial plan with a more sophisticated one. If the old planner also sold you investments, then the new planner will also review them and, no doubt, recommend changes. As already described, there can be significant costs associated with liquidating certain types of commission products.

Financial Representatives

If you have a small amount of assets, it may be necessary to replace representatives of one company with representatives from another company. Because these types of advisors sell products for commissions, your assets may not be easy to move due to the financial penalties or proprietary products. It all depends on the type of commission charged by the representative and the type of product.

You can expect substantial changes for your assets. The changes represent sales for the new advisor, and sales produce commissions. Because this is the only way that the advisor can be paid, you have to assume that this individual will replace as many of your current investments as possible.

SUMMARY

✔ You should subject all current professionals to the due diligence process that is described in this book. Never rely on advisor-controlled information when hiring advisors.

✔ Replacing advisors should not be taken lightly. You want a beneficial process that minimizes lost performance, expense, and time delays.

✔ Do not terminate advisors for the wrong reasons. It is not right to blame an advisor for negative returns in a down market.

✔ All terminations due to insufficient results should be based on relative performance and risk measurements.

✔ The number one strategy used by advisors who are fighting terminations is to buy time that can be used to correct the problems.

✔ Ethical lapses on the part of the advisor are grounds for immediate termination.

✔ Do not fall into the trap of replacing advisors every few years. You are losing time and performance. Find a quality advisor and stay with this individual.

11

RELATIONSHIPS

Why do so many smart people retain weak financial advisors for such extended periods of time? Knowing the answer is critical if you are going to maximize your asset amounts for retirement. The core of the issue is the relationship that advisors develop with you.

We already know that money is a very emotional topic for most people. We also know that Wall Street has trained hundreds of thousands of advisors to use those emotions to sell its products. For example, when we feel optimistic, Wall Street sells us equity products and when we are fearful it sells us fixed annuities, CDs, and money market funds.

Emotional attachment to your assets and the desire for financial security is being used against you to enhance the revenues and profits of the industry. Financial advisors are at the heart of this process and they use personal relationships as a way to achieve their needs for producing revenue and income.

The following are a few observations from my 26 years in the industry. They explain why investors frequently stay with weak advisors:

- You do not know the right questions to ask during and after the selection process to determine the quality of an advisor.
- You are swayed by a sales presentation that made the professional sound like the world's greatest living expert on investing.
- You are so blinded by the relationship with the advisor that you have lost sight of what should be its only real purpose—the achievement of your financial goals.
- You delegated so much influence to the advisor that you are no longer in control of your financial future.
- You are so dependent on the advisor that you are afraid to make a change.
- You will have to allocate time to replacing a weak advisor, and you are a busy person.
- You do not know how to select a better advisor, so the easier choice is to stay with the one you have.
- You are a procrastinator and always have other activities that take precedence over planning for your financial future.

Three issues are at the heart of my observations: knowledge, time, and relationships. The purpose of this book is to provide the knowledge you need to select a high-quality advisor. You have already committed a few hours to reading the book. Now you must use the knowledge that you acquired to find the best advisor you can for your assets.

Developing a long-term relationship with a quality advisor is the outcome of following the Principles described in this book. The critical difference between the past and the future is you are entering into the relationship for the right reasons because you control the process.

Perception May Not Be Reality

There is a perception among investors that all advisors are experts at investing; investors reason they would not be licensed professionals otherwise. This perception causes many investors to turn their assets over to advisors who may have a few weeks of experience and who may never have even graduated from high school—both are possibilities, because the industry has no minimum standards for experience or education.

The perception that all advisors are experts is flawed. The majority of advisors are not skilled investment professionals—they are sales representatives. Your perceptions are based on company advertising and finely honed sales presentations which are designed to sell you on the advisor. When they win your assets, they also win your confidence, and at that point, they are in a position to influence your future investment decisions. All they have to know is more than you for you to consider them experts. As such, the less you know, the easier it is for a representative with a minimal amount of knowledge or experience to win your trust.

The real problem is that you may end up selecting any self-professed expert who passes a subjective screening process.

It Is a Business

Should you have a personal relationship with a professional who is advising you on decisions that will determine your financial future? The answer is "no." You want a business relationship focused on achieving your financial goals. However, this defies the way that people interact with one another. People connect with others through personal relationships—just about everyone wants more friends. However, when a relationship is used against you to win and retain assets for the wrong reasons, you must rethink it. Has the relationship gotten too personal? Has it blinded you to certain realities? Is it interfering with the achievement of your financial goals?

What you should always remember is that for the advisor, relationships are part of a business strategy that was developed to win your assets. This does not mean that advisors are bad people; it simply means that they have to make a living. The advisor develops and manages relationships as part of the sales process, but the investor takes relationships personally.

The issue is not whether the advisor is a nice person. The individual whom you hire could be exceptionally nice. Niceness, however, does not equal competence and integrity, which is what you need to achieve your goals.

Dependency

The less you know, the more dependent you are on the financial services industry for information and advice. This is the number one reason why low-quality advisors can make good livings selling you financial products. You do not know enough to recognize their deficiencies, if information was deliberately withheld from you, if the quality of their services is poor, or if the results they produce are substandard. You hope that the quality is there and, when it is not, you eventually find another professional to advise you—usually after a number of underperforming years. Your lack of knowledge makes you easy prey for an industry that engenders dependency and then takes advantage of it.

Dependency is the foundation of the strong personal relationships that you develop with financial advisors. Dependency also explains the long-term nature of these relationships and your reluctance to make changes. You do not want to start over with new relationships unless you absolutely must. The result is that a high percentage of investors stay in bad advisor relationships much longer than they should.

You know from frequent newspaper headlines that the financial services industry is one of the most conflicted in the country—too much money tempts insufficient integrity on a daily basis. Even with this knowledge, you place your financial future in the industry's hands and hope that the results are there to justify your trust. This is the ultimate dependency: you trust an industry that has a history of being untrustworthy.

What real choice do you have? The markets are complex and volatile, and they produce extraordinary volumes of information that must be processed to make quality investment decisions. You can choose to do the work yourself or turn the responsibility over to professionals. According to our research, 84 percent of investors with meaningful assets choose the latter strategy due to their limited time or knowledge. As a result, a hazardous relationship is allowed to perpetuate itself based on your need for advice.

Time Is Precious

Time is one of those precious commodities which we all lack. After deducting work hours, family hours, and personal hours from the week, it seems that there is little time even to sleep. Spending your time replacing a weak financial advisor is no doubt low on your priority list. You have to terminate the current advisor, evaluate alternatives, select a new professional, and go through the start-up cycle.

The financial services industry is very aware of the time constraints that impact your life. Those in the industry know that the vast majority of all investors do not take the time to learn what they need to know in order to invest their own assets. Most investors will not even take the time to read the service agreements that will determine services and expense for their assets. Instead, they base trust on gut instincts, because it minimizes the time that they must commit to the process. This opens the door for sales representatives to win by being personable and telling investors what they want to hear.

Fear of the Unknown

Investors tend to fear what they do not understand. This plays into the hands of some financial service companies that deliberately keep you in the dark so you will not question the advice delivered by their representatives. The less you understand, the easier it is to sell you junk products for inflated commissions. On the one hand, you have no one to blame but yourself. You could have taken the time to educate yourself, but did not. However, the industry is also to blame because it uses your fear against you to achieve its goals.

Fear of Change

Too many investors are afraid of change, so they stay with advisors they know—even when these advisors do not have the competence or integrity to help them achieve their goals. It is the devil you know versus the devil you do not know. Investors resist change because it may force them to go outside their comfort zone. They are frozen in the status quo, like the proverbial deer in the headlights, even when their current situation is not working and they know it. Whatever the reason might be for resistance to change, it puts investors' financial futures in serious jeopardy.

Confrontation

A significant percentage of the population does not like confrontation, but this is what happens when you criticize the results produced by the advisor—you are confronting the advisor about missed expectations. The advisor will spend as much time as you allow defending performance—after all, it is easier to keep an existing client than to find a new one. Sometimes there is no way for an investor to avoid addressing the problem head-on. Confronting your advisor is what you need to do if you want to improve a bad situation.

Apathy Is Dangerous

Change starts with a personal desire to improve your financial future. However, many investors are content to maintain the status quo because they do not appreciate the financial benefits of change. Too many investors are not motivated enough to overcome the uncertainty that accompanies change. Their comments illustrate this apathy:

- "My advisor is doing an adequate job."
- "My advisor is a friend of mine, so I know I can trust him."
- "I do not know my results, but I think they are OK."

The danger of apathy is twofold. First, you tend to ignore what is happening to your assets and rely on what the advisor tells you. Second, apathy encourages procrastination, which causes you to put off actions that you should take now.

Far too many investors believe that underperformance is tomorrow's problem, which makes procrastination easy. Investors say that they will wait until the end of the year to review investment results, but when the end of the year comes, they decide to wait a little longer. Deferral means not having to deal with issues now, but these issues will not be any simpler to deal with in the future. In fact, they become increasingly complex, because the clock is ticking. Every year of underperformance is another year of improved returns that is lost forever.

Hope Springs Eternal

Every year during spring training, 30 baseball teams hope to win the World Series. However, there are only a few teams that have a relatively strong chance of winning, even though the world is full of over-achievers. This reality notwithstanding, avid fans support their team even if they know at the beginning of the season that their team is going to have a losing record.

The same can be said for financial advisors. Only a few have the credentials and integrity to help you achieve your goals. Most advisors are not capable of providing this level of service. However, you stay with weak advisors a lot longer than you should for the same reason that you root for a team that has no chance of winning the World Series: you keep hoping this will be your year. Why? Because the advisor told you last year that this year would be better. Even when there is ample evidence that your assets are lagging, you may give the advisor one more year, and then another year, and so on. Hope springs eternal, as they say. This is another major reason why bad advisors are retained for so long.

Daniel Kahneman, a Princeton psychologist and winner of the 2002 Nobel Prize in economic sciences describes our natural optimism this way: "We are not just optimistic, we are highly optimistic. And not only do we accentuate the positive, we often eliminate the negative. That is, we are overoptimistic while denying and minimizing potential problems—until after they bite us."

Influence Is Control

The industry makes you the decision maker for your assets and says that its professionals are "just" advisors who analyze alternatives and make recommendations. Two critical variables are the source of this sales pitch. First, advisors believe that they can avoid fiduciary liability for their advice when you are the decision maker. Second, they do not need to be in the role of decision maker to take control of your assets. If advisors can gain your trust, their ability to influence your decisions is the same as control. Whether they recommended one money manager or five, they controlled your decisions by controlling your choices.

Make no mistake: when you follow the advice of professionals, their influence is tantamount to control. After all, you did not hire an expert to be indecisive.

Whose Needs Come First

You look at your assets and see a quality education for your children, a future vacation home in the mountains, or a comfortable retirement when you reach age 65. Your advisor looks at your assets and sees a way to make the mortgage payment, the car payment, or a vacation to Hawaii. These very different views of your assets are at the core of the many conflicts that impact your relationships with advisors.

These are your assets, and your financial needs come well ahead of your advisor's need for income. Because this is a business relationship and not a personal one, your agreement with the professional should be based solely on the achievement of your financial goals. If your objectives are met, then it is no problem if the advisor earns a good living from your assets.

One Financial Future

You have one financial future and a fixed amount of time to generate assets for that future. When personal relationships distort your view, they have the potential to destroy that future. The damage occurs when you stay with low-quality professionals who deliver poor recommendations for your assets. Each year, you fall further behind, but the advisor's relationship skills cause you to retain the individual longer than you should.

Eventually you will run out of time to compound the returns you need to achieve your financial goals. Then all you can do is "create" additional time by delaying your retirement or working part-time. Suffice it to say that you will pay a severe penalty for staying with the wrong advisor for excessive periods of time because you have one financial future, and there is no way to turn the clock back.

There Is Only One Solution

You cannot expect the industry to reform itself until there are enough knowledgeable investors who only select quality advisors. When your selection process begins to impact their bottom lines, then companies will be motivated to reevaluate the quality of their advisors and their strategies for generating revenue. As I have said throughout this book, only investors can be the catalyst for this change. The more investors who put the Paladin Principles in Chapter Twelve to work for themselves the better, so tell your family members, friends, and associates about this book. Then and only then will the industry reform itself, because it will be in its best interest. Until such time, it is up to you to protect your financial future.

The Paladin Principles

The 17 Paladin Principles are the foundation of the knowledge contained in this book. Each Principle is important; collectively, they will dramatically increase your ability to select a quality advisor. The book also has an associated website, *www.paladinprinciples.com*, that was developed to make it even easier for you to use the Principles to find, evaluate, and monitor quality investment professionals.

The First Step

The first step of any journey is always the toughest. It is the step which overcomes the inertia that, when left unchallenged, will prevent you from achieving your goals. There will always be reasons to do nothing, and that may be your biggest challenge—to start a process that has a long-term consequence. It is like saving small amounts of money now so you will have a large sum later. However, when $10,000 becomes $100,000 and then $500,000, you will see the wisdom of that first step.

The Easier Way to Improve Results

Improving the quality of your advisor is the easiest and fastest way for you to improve the performance of your assets. The professional selection process is infinitely easier to learn than investing your own assets in the securities markets. All you have to do is follow the Principles described in this book and the due diligence process described in Chapter Six. The result? Increased assets for the rest of your life.

SUMMARY

- ✔ The financial services industry wants you to be dependent on the advisors who sell its products. It facilitates the sales process and reduces their cost structure.

- ✔ It may be a personal relationship to you, but it is a business relationship to the advisor, who makes his or her living from your assets.

- ✔ You will have to spend time to improve the quality of advice that you receive for your assets. If you do not spend time now, you will have to do so later when you continue working full-time or part-time after your anticipated retirement date.

- ✔ Many investors are intimidated by changing advisors because they want to avoid confrontation. They sacrifice their financial futures rather than take necessary action steps.

- ✔ Most investors are apathetic about their financial futures due to lack of knowledge. They do not know how to pick securities, money managers, or personal advisors so they make snap decisions based on their intuition—a formula for disaster. Many of these investors experienced disaster in the early 2000s.

- ✔ Hope springs eternal: investors hope that they have a quality advisor, they hope that they are properly invested, and they hope that they achieve their goals.

- ✔ The first step is always the toughest, but it may be the difference between golden years and years of financial insecurity.

12

THE PALADIN PRINCIPLES

I developed the 17 Paladin Principles for one reason: to change the way you select personal financial advisors for your assets. Change is critical if you want to achieve financial goals, especially goals that impact your retirement years. This chapter provides you with a description of each Principle, why it is important, and the impact it can have on your financial future.

If you follow these Principles, you will be able to avoid low-quality advisors whose primary interest is maximizing their incomes from your assets. You will be able to select a competent, trustworthy professional who has the knowledge to be your coordinator and gatekeeper and who helps you realize your financial goals.

Many of the benefits of the Principles may not be realized until later in life during your retirement years when you have more assets and increased financial security. Perhaps the biggest short-term benefit of a more objective approach for selecting an advisor is the ability to sleep better at night, knowing that your assets are in the hands of a quality professional whom you can trust.

THE 17 PALADIN PRINCIPLES

1 **You cannot control the volatility of the securities markets, but you can control the quality of your advisor.**

There is nothing you can do about the volatility of the stock market (except not invest in it). All you can do is mitigate this volatility by using a carefully planned investment strategy.

One source of risk that you have when you invest in the securities markets is the quality of advice that you receive from financial professionals who drive your strategy. You can do something about this risk. Just as you need a smart investment plan, you also need a sound process for selecting a high-quality advisor. By choosing a good advisor, you will receive competent advice that will reduce the volatility of your investments.

If you cannot change the market, then change the quality of advice that you receive while investing in the market.

2 **Learning to select a quality advisor is easier than learning to invest your own assets.**

This entire book is based on the premise that you cannot invest assets on your own and expect to achieve the same returns as a competent, trustworthy advisor. The markets are too complex, volatile, and time-consuming. Therefore, you must possess substantial amounts of specialized knowledge and time to be successful. If you do not have sufficient amounts of these two key ingredients, you are among the 84 percent of investors who use the services of personal financial advisors.

Can you achieve your financial goals with an incompetent professional advising you? Can you achieve your goals with an untrustworthy professional influencing or controlling your decisions? In both cases, your financial future would be compromised by the professional whom you select as your advisor.

Changing advisors every few years is the consequence of not knowing how to select a quality professional. However, change is a symptom of an underlying problem. When an advisor does not meet your goals, you terminate the individual's services. Perhaps you use a subjective process for selecting a replacement. A few years later, you repeat the replacement process until you eventually are unable to achieve your goals because you have run out of time.

You must learn a new process for selecting advisors that will produce the desired result: competent, trustworthy advice. Once you have learned to select a quality advisor, you will compound higher returns over longer time periods and increase the probability of achieving your goals.

3 **Do not allow apathy to undermine your financial future.**

Apathy is a major obstacle for too many investors. They do not understand the complex investment process, so they turn their assets over to any advisor who seems competent. They leave their assets with this low-quality sales professional for prolonged periods of time. Their rationale for doing nothing is that doing something takes time and knowledge which they do not have; besides, how do they know that the new advisor will be any better than the current one? Investors use the fact that there are no guarantees in life as an excuse to do nothing.

Apathy implies that you do not care about the results produced by the advisor—"after all," you might say, "there is always next year." Our research indicates that nothing could be further from the truth. It is not that you do not care. Intuitively, you know that you need a quality professional to help you achieve your goals. It is simply that you do not know how to find, evaluate, and monitor advisors. Now you do, though—you have read this book.

4 **Spend a small amount of time now so that you save a lot of time later.**

Understanding the need for quality advice is critical, but nothing will happen unless you take the time to improve your situation.

The time commitment is not months, weeks, or even days. It will only take a few hours for you to obtain the information you need to improve the quality of your life during retirement—no more than the time it takes to read this book.

Increasing your knowledge is the first step. The second step is the time that it takes to find, evaluate, and hire the professional you will depend on, perhaps for the rest of your life. Think of it as the horse and the cart. The horse is the knowledge that enables you to select a quality advisor. The cart is the application of the knowledge in the selection process. You need the horse in front of the cart, and you must commit time to both.

You can spend the necessary time now—or you can spend it later, when you do not have enough assets to retire and maintain your preferred standard of living. Instead of retiring in comfort, you will have to continue working part-time or full-time to make ends meet. It makes more sense to set aside a small amount of time now rather than a lot of years later.

5 **Make sure you select advisors for their qualifications and not their personalities.**

Too many investors say they hired a particular advisor because the professional was a nice person. Unfortunately, this nice person was also incompetent and suffered from lapses of integrity. In fact, being nice was part of the advisor's sales strategy for winning assets. This is a popular strategy for professionals because they know that many investors use a subjective, intuitive process for selecting advisors—"nice" sells.

The unfortunate reality is that personalities have nothing to do with competence or integrity; they may be nothing more than sales techniques. An advisor's friendly demeanor is the foundation for building a relationship with you, the investor. It is important to understand that niceness is a positive character trait that has nothing to do with helping you achieve your goals.

There is also a counterpoint to the "nice sells" philosophy. Some of the very best consultants in the country do not have strong sales skills or outgoing personalities. They are more thoughtful, analytical, quantitative types of professionals who spend their day working with data that impacts the performance of your assets. They are highly competent advisors with excellent integrity ratings but relatively subdued personalities, and they are exactly the type of professional whom you want advising you on the investment of your assets.

6 Utilize an objective, rational process for selecting an advisor that is not affected by emotions or sales skills.

Your advisor must possess two critical qualities: integrity and competence. Integrity lets you trust the individual's advice. Competence means that the advice is of sufficient quality for you to achieve your financial goals. You cannot evaluate these qualities utilizing an intuitive process that relies on advisor-controlled inputs.

Money is a very emotional topic, especially if your assets or revenue streams are inadequate for your current or future needs. Wall Street has developed a very sophisticated sales process for taking advantage of emotions that facilitate the distribution of its products. For example, it appeals to your need for performance by selling a "hot" mutual fund—even when there is substantial evidence that the fund will not produce the same high returns in the future. The sales pitch is designed to appeal to your need for higher returns, even though the promise of such returns is questionable.

You must recognize that emotions are not your friend when it comes to achieving your financial goals. In fact, your emotions open the door to sales processes designed to evoke emotion-backed decisions. Rational thought and objectivity go out the window, and you are under the control of the advisor.

Objectivity helps you make a better decision by minimizing the impact of the advisor's selling skills. For example, you can replace the professional's sales presentation with a questionnaire that is designed to obtain the information you need to make a quality decision.

There is no doubt that intuition is the easy way to hire advisors for your assets, because there is a very low time commitment. All you have to do is listen to a few sales presentations and choose the one you like the best. Be aware, though, that intuition also represents the riskiest way to select advisors. If you go with your gut instincts, you have a much higher probability of selecting unqualified professionals.

7 Make sure you have complete information before selecting a professional to be your advisor.

Determining the integrity and competence of professionals is impossible if you rely on the input that they control. Advisors only provide information that makes them look good. As a result, just about all advisors will leave out any information that might cause you to exclude them from your selection process. As you might imagine, though, this is the most important information for you to have.

Obtaining complete information is the most critical step in the selection process for several reasons:

- Advisor-controlled information is incomplete.
- Incomplete information leads to a bad decision.
- A bad selection decision will cost you time and performance from which it is difficult to recover.
- You are destined to repeat a dysfunctional selection process every few years unless you take control of the information you rely on to make a decision.

8 Require all-important advisor information to be in writing.

In addition to obtaining complete due diligence information, it is also critical that the information be in writing and certified by the advisor that it is complete and accurate. Once it is in written form, the advisor has lost control over it, which impacts them two ways. First, they cannot deny later what they provided you; second, advisors know that you may turn the information over to a supervisor, the regulators, or an attorney. For these reasons, there is a high probability that you will receive accurate information when it is in writing.

This permanent record also screens out advisors who resist providing written information. They may want you to rely exclusively on their verbal sales presentations because they know that verbal information is easy to deny later when it is your word against theirs. An old adage that bears repeating is "trust what you see, not what you hear."

9   **Permit no exceptions to your due diligence process.**

Most car accidents occur within four miles of home when you are less vigilant due to the familiarity of your surroundings. The same holds true when selecting advisors you know—acquaintances, friends, and family members. You may be inclined to let your guard down because you have an established personal relationship with the advisor.

Familiarity may cause you to bypass the due diligence process when you think you know the advisor, especially if the professional is a nice person or was referred to you by someone you trust. Unfortunately, the individual may be incompetent or may not have the integrity that you require in an advisor. You may conjure up any number of reasons for bypassing the due diligence process, but in all cases, the reasons put your financial future at risk.

10   **Require full disclosure about all potential conflicts of interest.**

A minimum requirement of your advisor is full and complete disclosure about all potential conflicts that impact your financial future. Only then can you turn your financial future over to a professional with a reasonable amount of certainty that your interests come first.

Any advisor who refuses to provide full disclosure must be automatically excluded from your selection process because you have to assume that the professional has something to hide. It may be a minor issue or a major one, but whatever it is, the advisor wants it to be kept secret.

The paradox is that this same advisor expects you to divulge everything there is to know about your personal situation and hand over your financial future. If the advisor wants full disclosure from you, he or she should be willing to provide full disclosure in return. Four primary areas require full disclosure: compliance record, competence, compensation, and conflicts of interest.

11 **Verify integrity by reviewing the advisor's compliance record.**

How can you commit your financial future to a professional until you know (as best you can) that the professional is worthy of your trust? There is only one answer. You must evaluate integrity by checking the advisor's compliance record.

Even the National Association of Securities Dealers says that you should review the compliance records of professionals before investing your assets with them. You will see any client complaints and regulatory actions in their records. An advisor with numerous complaints should be avoided.

Do not make the mistake of relying on references to evaluate trustworthiness, because they are very easy to manipulate. For example, you may be talking to the advisor's brother-in-law, friend, or a coached client. Professionals will never give you a reference that makes them look bad. There may be reasons to talk to references; however, verifying integrity is not one of them.

12 **Verify competence by evaluating education and experience.**

After integrity, competence is the other critical advisor characteristic. The foundation of competence is the knowledge that professionals have accumulated from education and experience. Knowledge is the source for competent advice and there is no substitute for it. Either the advisor has sufficient knowledge to help you achieve your goals or the advisor does not. In the absence of substantial advisor knowledge, you are in real trouble, because incompetent advice combined with volatile markets will destroy your financial future.

This part of your due diligence process must therefore be focused on two variables: education and experience. Education is a critical building block for the accumulation of knowledge. The education can be acquired in school, through continuing education programs, certification programs, and memberships in associations that emphasize continuing education.

Experience is the school of hard knocks. Due to the complexity of the markets, newer advisors make numerous mistakes with investors' assets and learn from those mistakes so they can produce better results in the future. This is the number one reason why you want experienced professionals advising you—let them make their mistakes with other investors' assets.

Education and experience are the dynamic duo when it comes to competence.

13 **You must be the advisor's only source of compensation.**

The financial services industry is built on a culture of selling products, not providing value-added advice. Advisors are paid substantial amounts of money to sell securities, mutual funds, annuities, life insurance, limited partnerships, and other financial products. A consequence of this culture is its focus on generating revenue for companies and income for advisors. The achievement of your goals is secondary.

This sales culture thrives, even as you read this book, for two primary reasons. First, billions of dollars of compensation are paid to 650,000 advisors each year for selling financial products. The source of payment is the thousands of companies that manufacture the products, including companies that also distribute their own products. Commissions are the financial incentive to sell their products, not deliver quality advice to you.

The second reason that this culture thrives is investors' continued willingness to buy products that compensate advisors with commissions. Perhaps one day, all investors will demand fee-based advice, this culture will die, and it will be replaced by one that is friendlier to their interests. In the final analysis, investors let this culture continue to flourish when they buy commission products.

At the core of the problem is relationships and trust. The industry is very adept at building trusting relationships and using the trust to sell its products. If you want to minimize this major source of conflict, then you have to be the professional's sole source of compensation, and there is only one way to do that. You must pay fees, not commissions, for the services that you use to achieve your financial goals.

14 **Quarterly performance reports are a mandatory service.**

Each quarter you must review a performance report that documents the results of your advisor and the recommended managers compared to applicable indices and benchmarks. This vital information determines the overall effectiveness of the advisor's strategy for helping you achieve your goals. In the absence of this report, you are traveling to a destination in the dark with no way to measure progress.

Do not confuse performance reports and brokerage statements—they are not the same. Statements display the market value of assets at the end of each month and transactions that include buys, sells, and receipt of income. The typical brokerage statement does not even display cost data, much less performance information because the industry does not want you to know your actual returns. If you did, you might terminate your current service provider. Once again, the industry is betting that less information (when you do not know performance or the relationship between cost and market) protects its interests.

All "real" financial consultants provide quarterly performance reports. It is the primary service that warrants the payment of an ongoing fee. The reports are an early warning system about performance problems and other issues that can undermine the achievement of your goals. In addition, they bring peace of mind because you have learned to trust what you see, not what you hear.

However, financial representatives rarely provide performance reports for one or more of three reasons:

1. They do not have a system that produces the reports.
2. They do not want you to know your performance history. Investors who are kept in the dark have higher retention rates than investors who know their results.
3. They do not have an ongoing revenue stream that offsets the expense of the performance reports.

Regardless of the reason, you should never entrust your assets to an advisor who cannot provide quarterly performance reports.

15   Ignoring a red flag is hazardous to your financial future.

Advisors either have sufficient knowledge to help you achieve your goals or they do not. They either tell the truth or they do not. They either place your interests ahead of theirs or they do not. Competence and integrity are not gray areas that are subject to negotiation. However, they are difficult to identify and measure; most investors take them for granted or ignore them. This is the reason why red flags are so important.

A red flag is something that creates concern in you about the quality of the professionals' advice or their integrity. For example, you become aware that money market funds recommended by the advisor have exceptionally high management fees—more than double the rates of comparable funds. Then you discover that the advisor is paid a portion of the fee to market the funds. This is a major red flag.

Another red flag occurs when advisors limit your choices to particular products. You may never know the real reason for the limitation; however, all you have to know is that limitation is bad. Someone is benefiting, and it is not you. You have received a warning that the advisor's recommendations are tainted.

A red flag is important because it may be the tip of the proverbial iceberg—you just do not know. How can you entrust your financial future to an advisor who did not disclose a material fact? That this individual was paid to sell a particular money market fund with excessive expenses? The answer is that you cannot. The advisor chose to take advantage of your lack of knowledge by assuming you would not find out about the revenue sharing from the fund. The safest strategy for you is to assume that there may be other breaches of trust you do not about and terminate the relationship immediately.

Always pay attention to red flags. You may only get one warning.

16 **Minimize the personal relationship with your advisor.**

You have friends, associates, and acquaintances. Your financial advisor most likely falls into one of these three categories. However, the people whom you know are not in a position to impact your financial future the way that investment professionals are. In addition, because advisors know the most intimate details of your financial life, it is easy for them to develop close personal relationships with you. Less scrupulous advisors use the relationship to take advantage of you.

There are several important reasons why it is dangerous to have too close a relationship with an advisor.

- Relationships facilitate the use of the advisor's sales skills— which are tactics for winning and retaining your assets.
- Your objectivity declines when you have a personal relationship with an advisor.
- Advisors who are friends are more difficult to terminate; as a result, you may put up with a mediocre relationship a lot longer than you should.
- You may be reluctant to ask tough questions of a professional whom you consider a friend.
- Whereas you might be skeptical about strangers, you risk making faulty positive assumptions about friends.

The bottom line is that this particular relationship benefits the professional more than you. It can put your financial future at risk.

17 Always interview multiple advisors so you have a choice.

One of the best ways to protect your financial future is to never limit your advisor candidates to just one. This is good for the advisor because there is no competition, but it is bad for you because your choices are limited. You gain perspective when you interview several advisors and can use it to identify positive and negative characteristics. When advisors compete for your business, you win—they will tend to do their best work, offer higher levels of service, and may even propose lower fees.

If you limit your choice to one advisor, you run a significant risk of selecting an advisor with a great sales pitch. You liked what the individual had to say, so why look any further? Because your goal is to hire the best advisor you can find and make that individual responsible for your financial future.

Congratulations!

You now know more about evaluating, selecting, and retaining advisors than most of the investors who use the services of investment professionals. This knowledge will benefit you for the rest of your life. It is also important to note that your increased knowledge is the beginning of the journey, not the end. Step one was to buy the book and step two was to read it. The third step (and the most important one) is to use the information to dramatically improve the quality of professional on whom you depend for investment advice. Then your dream of a secure financial future will become a reality.

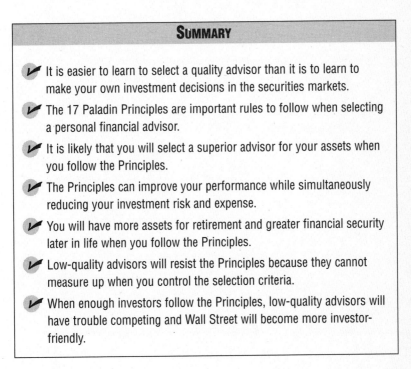

SUMMARY

- ✔ It is easier to learn to select a quality advisor than it is to learn to make your own investment decisions in the securities markets.
- ✔ The 17 Paladin Principles are important rules to follow when selecting a personal financial advisor.
- ✔ It is likely that you will select a superior advisor for your assets when you follow the Principles.
- ✔ The Principles can improve your performance while simultaneously reducing your investment risk and expense.
- ✔ You will have more assets for retirement and greater financial security later in life when you follow the Principles.
- ✔ Low-quality advisors will resist the Principles because they cannot measure up when you control the selection criteria.
- ✔ When enough investors follow the Principles, low-quality advisors will have trouble competing and Wall Street will become more investor-friendly.

EPILOGUE

There are at least 60,000 advisors in America, out of 650,000, who have the competence and integrity you need to achieve your goals. That is very good news. The bad news is there are close to 600,000 advisors who do not have these critical characteristics. Your challenge is to tell them apart. That is a daunting task because a high percentage of the lower quality advisors have excellent sales skills, and appear to be much better than they really are. This is the number one reason why I developed the Paladin Principles. The Principles provide rules and a process for making sure the advisor you select has the credentials and integrity you need to help achieve your goals.

Given all of the negative publicity about conflicts of interest, breaches of trust, and outright fraud, what choices are left for an investor? Is it to become your own advisor or money manager? Is it to hire an advisor who may be incompetent and untrustworthy? Or, is it to adopt a process that will help you select one of the 60,000 quality advisors? There really is no choice if you need financial advice to help you invest your assets. You must find the best possible advisor for your assets using the Paladin Principles.

The most immediate impact of the Paladin Principles is the reduced risk in selecting the wrong advisor. The Principles are designed to screen out those advisors and reveal their weaknesses. The result is an increased probability that you will choose a quality advisor.

You might also be asking yourself, "Is it really that bad?" and "Is it worth the extra time it could take to conduct an objective selection process?" After all, there is no guarantee the new advisor will be better than the old advisor. The answer is there are no guarantees, but there is an increased probability you will avoid weak advisors and select a qualified one. In addition, your time will be well spent because a quality advisor will have a dramatic effect on your assets. You can spend a little time now, or a lot of time later when you have insufficient assets for a quality retirement.

The reason is very simple. High quality advisors produce better results than low quality advisors. Better results produce hundreds of thousands of additional dollars for your retirement years. In addition, the results are delivered with lower risk and expense characteristics. For example, let us suppose the stock market is up 14 percent in 2003. A lower quality advisor produces a 10 percent return; a higher quality advisor produces an 18 percent return. One lagged the market return by 4 percent while the other outperformed it by the same amount. Compound that 8 percent difference over longer time-periods and you will have a substantial amount of additional dollars to fund your dreams of a quality retirement.

Another reason why you should adopt the Paladin Principles is you will have increased control over your financial future by reducing your dependence on Wall Street's advisors. When your knowledge level is low, your dependency is high, and that is the perfect environment for the abusive sales tactics of the financial industry. The less you know, the easier it is for advisors to win your trust and sell you low quality investments. Your best defenses are knowledge and an objective process that will weed out low quality advisors and products. As long as you have the discipline to adhere to the Principles, your odds of avoiding low quality advisors and selecting high quality advisors are greatly enhanced.

The high quality advisor you are seeking has the knowledge and resources to develop sophisticated investment strategies that will produce the results you need for lower levels of risk. As you might imagine, lower quality advisors sell you inferior products and your exposure to excess risk is an unnecessary consequence of their sales processes. Competent, trustworthy advisors can show you alternative strategies and help you select the one that is most suitable for your situation.

The right advisor can also produce investment solutions that have lower expense characteristics. For example, the advisor may recommend passive managers for certain asset classes that are more efficiently priced by the market. After all, why pay higher fees for active management when there is a low probability of the manager beating the index performance that is provided by a passive manager? Competent advisors understand these trade-offs and know how to structure solutions that minimize both risk and expense.

When it comes to comfort nothing is more important than being well informed. High quality advisors provide performance reports that document the most recent quarter's returns as well as year-to-date, and up to five years of historical results. These critical reports provide the data you need to determine your level of satisfaction with the managers recommended by the advisor. In the absence of these reports, you would have to develop your own performance monitoring system to track results or because you really do not know, and "hope" everything is satisfactory.

Quality advisors, sophisticated solutions, and performance reports produce another important benefit—sleeping better at night. Can you imagine the stress associated with approaching your retirement years with insufficient assets? Perhaps you are already living that nightmare. Can you afford to retire? Will you need a part-time job to make ends meet? Will you run out of money late in life when it is impossible to replace? Will you end up living on handouts from your children? The constant worry of insufficient assets can be minimized when you know a competent, trustworthy professional is helping you make decisions and is monitoring the results that are produced by your managers.

There are also intangible benefits when you utilize the Paladin Principles for the selection of advisors. One of the most important is helping change the Wall Street business model from selling to advising; this is what investors need to achieve their goals. The financial industry must receive a strong message that the days of its abusive sales practices are over. It will take a critical mass of investors using the Paladin Principles to make sure the message is heard loud and clear. A message that says investors want information they can trust from competent professionals who put the needs of their clients ahead of their need for income.

When enough investors use the Paladin Principles, Wall Street will get the message that the old business model will not work anymore—at least for knowledgeable investors. They will either develop business models that are friendly to investors or they will suffer the consequences in the form of reduced revenue and profit. Those financial companies that adopt positive business models will flourish because they will make it easy for knowledgeable investors to select their advisors.

We have also made it easy for you to use the Principles by developing a website that is based on the evaluation process described in this book. *paladinprinciples.com* provides several value-added services that will help you achieve your goals. For example:

- A Request For Information (RFI) has already been built including the disclosure documents, interview guide, and a Creed that advisors sign outlining their commitments to you.
- A learning center will continue your education until you are truly in control of your financial future.
- Tips are given to help you improve performance, reduce risk, and reduce expenses.
- There are also premium services based on Paladin professionals completing certain work for you.

In addition to the above functionalities, several additional high value services make the evaluation and monitoring of your advisor easier. For example:

- A Registry of Advisors helps you find an advisor in your city. You can review profiles and complete the RFI process while still maintaining your anonymity.
- A service, that is the only one of its kind, will help you monitor the performance of your advisor on a quarterly basis. You can also build a track record of your advisor's results over time—make sure the professional is producing results that are competitive with your alternatives. This early warning system enables you to limit the impact of bad advice on the performance of your assets.
- A similar service will also monitor the compliance record of advisors after you have selected them.
- You can also join a Paladin Chapter in your community to continue your education and share information with other members

Now that you have finished reading the book, you are at a crossroads. Do you continue increasing your knowledge base so you can have even greater control over your financial future? Do you apply the Principles to your current advisors to verify their competency and integrity? Do you use the information and services available to you to select a new advisor? Or, do you file the information into the "interesting" category and continue down the same path you have been on for several years? The choices are yours. I have provided the information you need to make a dramatic improvement in your financial future. Now it is up to you to use the information. I hope you take advantage of the opportunity that has been presented to you in *Who's Watching Your Money?*

INDEX